Table of Contents

Copyright © Mometrix Media. You have been licensed one copy of this document for personal use only.
Any other reproduction or redistribution is strictly prohibited. All rights reserved.

Top 20 Test Taking Tips

1. Carefully follow all the test registration procedures
2. Know the test directions, duration, topics, question types, how many questions
3. Setup a flexible study schedule at least 3-4 weeks before test day
4. Study during the time of day you are most alert, relaxed, and stress free
5. Maximize your learning style; visual learner use visual study aids, auditory learner use auditory study aids
6. Focus on your weakest knowledge base
7. Find a study partner to review with and help clarify questions
8. Practice, practice, practice
9. Get a good night's sleep; don't try to cram the night before the test
10. Eat a well balanced meal
11. Know the exact physical location of the testing site; drive the route to the site prior to test day
12. Bring a set of ear plugs; the testing center could be noisy
13. Wear comfortable, loose fitting, layered clothing to the testing center; prepare for it to be either cold or hot during the test
14. Bring at least 2 current forms of ID to the testing center
15. Arrive to the test early; be prepared to wait and be patient
16. Eliminate the obviously wrong answer choices, then guess the first remaining choice
17. Pace yourself; don't rush, but keep working and move on if you get stuck
18. Maintain a positive attitude even if the test is going poorly
19. Keep your first answer unless you are positive it is wrong
20. Check your work, don't make a careless mistake

Copyright © Mometrix Media. You have been licensed one copy of this document for personal use only. Any other reproduction or redistribution is strictly prohibited. All rights reserved.

Case Management

Attorney misconduct

The statements from Rule 8.4 of the Model Rules of Professional Conduct define attorney misconduct as follows:

- It is misconduct for an attorney in law to violate or attempt to violate the Rules of Professional Conduct, assist or cajole others to do so.
- It is misconduct to commit a crime that negatively reflects on the attorney's honesty, trustworthiness, or professionalism.
- It is misconduct to engage in dishonest, fraudulent, or deceitful behavior.
- It is misconduct to practice and display prejudicial attitude towards the administration of justice.
- It is misconduct for an attorney in law to state or imply an ability to exercise an improper influence over a government agency or official.
- It is misconduct to assist a judge or judicial officer in violation of applicable rules of judicial conduct or other law.

Ethical issues

The following are some of the ethical issues investigative personnel may face:

- Confusion of role and duty by private and security investigators: concerns loyalty to clients, employers, and court.
- Violation of privacy in surveillance operations and undercover investigations.
- Disclosure of confidential information obtained during surveillance, undercover investigations, or recorded in victims' and witnesses' statements.
- Use of unethical methods, such as deception, intimate relationships, and coercion to obtain information, or the use of lies, threats, and intimidation during interviews and interrogations; intimacy with witnesses.
- Temptation to entrap suspects based on intrusion of emotions into the investigative process.
- Falsification of expenses, such as exaggeration of costs in order to gain larger profits.
- Managers' failure to take responsibility for consequences of undercover operations: unethical methods used as well as emotional condition of the agents may be ignored.
- Unethical treatment of informants: abuse, coercion of those who are close to being involved in illegal acts.

Conflict analysis

Factors that should be considered in conflict analysis are as follows:

- Level of interdependency – how much the conflicting parties need each other to maintain operations, to cooperate with others, or satisfy the needs of others. As the level of interdependency increases, so does the risk of conflict.
- Number of interested parties – number of individuals or groups who have an interest in the result of the conflict. The higher the number of parties, the more difficult it is to resolve the conflict.
- Constituent representation – the opposing parties may be representing interests of other parties who are not directly

Copyright © Mometrix Media. You have been licensed one copy of this document for personal use only. Any other reproduction or redistribution is strictly prohibited. All rights reserved.

involved in the conflict. It is more difficult to resolve a conflict with representatives.

- Level of negotiator's authority – conflict resolution is easier when the negotiator's level of authority is higher.
- Level of urgency – critical urgency usually means obstacles in reaching a consensus.
- Communication channels – synchronous, face-to-face communication methods produce better results.

Workplace conflicts

Workplace conflicts, especially those involving management, often result in lawsuits. Some of these lawsuits are rightful, many of them are not. The most common types of lawsuits provoked by workplace conflicts include retaliatory and frivolous. A retaliatory lawsuit is filed on the premise that the employer has taken negative measures against an employee who complained of discrimination or reported to the authorities an ongoing illegal activity within the company. Retaliatory lawsuits are usually filed by grudging employees who hope to inflict damage on the company and gain some financial benefits. Frivolous lawsuits can be defined as any complaints that are filed based not on the actual wrongdoing but on the assumption of the plaintiff that there is financial profit to be gained. These lawsuits in many instances are nothing short of legalized extortion.

Resulting in sabotage, harassment, and fraud

Workplace conflicts, which are ignored by the management and left unresolved, cause resentment and may provoke even law-abiding loyal employees to commit crimes such as theft, sabotage, and fraud. For example, if one employee is in charge of providing data for the other, but is late with his/her report, the other employee who has to use this data to further report to the management may feel irritation and anger. To vent off these feelings, the employee may decide to sabotage the work of the first employee to show that he/she should be blamed for any delays and avert the blame from him/herself. Unresolved personality conflicts may provoke employees to abuse their status and harass other employees who are lower in rank. Resentment at management may result in the employee's fraud to incriminate the manager.

Conflict resolution

Conflict resolution is a process of analyzing and eliminating a conflict situation by means of specific conflict resolution techniques. Effective conflict resolution techniques are designed to prevent conflicts before they break out. They usually focus on adequately addressing interests of each opposing party in order to achieve a result that satisfies all. Conflict resolution techniques may be direct and mediated. Direct conflict resolution implies negotiating the interests of both opposing parties weighing the interest against the working relationships concerned. Mediated conflict resolution may involve two or more opposing parties, and another party who views the situation from an impartial standpoint. In some cases, conflict resolution implies that the opposing parties just acknowledge their differences, but no action is taken to actually solve the dispute.

Conflict resolution methods include conciliation, mediation, arbitration, and litigation. Conciliation is a process of settling conflicts in a friendly manner without resorting to judicial means. Two opposing parties are brought together to reach a compromise to avoid taking a case

Copyright © Mometrix Media. You have been licensed one copy of this document for personal use only. Any other reproduction or redistribution is strictly prohibited. All rights reserved.

to trial. Mediation is a process of settling conflicts by involving an independent and impartial individual, a mediator, who helps the two opposing parties resolve their disagreement. Arbitration is a process of settling conflicts by submitting the dispute to an unbiased third person, referred to as arbitrator, designated by the opposing parties, who agree to comply with the decision to be made at a hearing where both parties will have an opportunity to present their case. Litigation is a process of settling conflicts by bringing a legal issue in court for a judicial contest in order to enforce a particular right.

Attorney-client fee conflict resolution

To avoid expensive and time-consuming fee conflicts between attorneys and their clients, some attorneys have begun furnishing the engagement letters and retention agreements with arbitration clauses. The attorney/client relationship does not form until both sides agree upon the terms of the engagement so there is no conflict of interest prohibition against the attorney discussing a mechanism of conflict resolution with the prospective client. The law allows for arbitration agreements as long as they do not bind the parties into unreasonable contracts. If the attorney does not provide an arbitration agreement it should be the client's decision to propose the arbitration to the lawyer. Similarly, businesses should propose arbitration as a means of resolving potential fee conflicts, as a carefully drafted conflict resolution clause could save the business and the attorney substantial time, cost, and aggravation.

ADR

Alternative Dispute Resolution (ADR) is a process of adjudicating disputes by means other than litigation. These means include arbitration, mediation, and mini-trials.

ADR is currently used in labor disputes, divorce actions, and personal injury claims. The key concept of the ADR is to increase motivation of all the parties and their lawyers to resolve the conflict without resorting to lawsuits. ADR is similar to litigation in terms of execution: there is a hearing where all the parties are given a chance to present their case, prove their case with evidence, and obtain a fair resolution. The difference is that ADR allows for more creativity in problem solving while litigation might require the parties to maintain the undesirable relationships.

Alternative conflict resolution methods can be used to resolve the following cases:
- Commercial and labor disputes, such as property disputes, small scale frauds, drug and alcohol abuse, sexual harassment, etc.
- Divorce actions
- Motor vehicle tort claims, such as accidents, property right violation, etc.
- Medical malpractice tort claims, such as misdiagnose, negligence, etc.

Main advantages of the alternative conflict resolution methods, such as conciliation, mediation, and arbitration, include:
- Low cost – it is not necessary for the conflicting parties to pay high attorney and court fees
- Short processing time – no need to wait for the long litigation process
- Easy execution – no need to fill out multiple papers, collect and submit numerous documents.

The Administrative Dispute Resolution Act of 1996 offers the following guidelines for agencies to promote alternative means of conflict resolution:

- 7 -

Copyright © Mometrix Media. You have been licensed one copy of this document for personal use only. Any other reproduction or redistribution is strictly prohibited. All rights reserved.

- Developing a policy that addresses the use of alternative means of conflict resolution and case management.
- Consulting with the agency designated to facilitate and encourage the use of alternative conflict resolution. The agency must be qualified under section 573 of title 5, United States Code.
- Applying alternative means of conflict resolution in a) formal and informal hearings aimed at resolving disputes; b) creation of rules, regulations, and polices; c) enforcement actions; d) issuing and revoking licenses or permits; e) administration of contracts; f) lawsuits brought by or against the agency.

The alternative means of conflict resolution should not be used in the following cases:
- The unique nature of the conflict requires a definitive and authoritative manner of resolution in order to create a precedent.
- The conflict may involve the Government policy and require additional procedures before reaching a final resolution.
- The conflict resolution requires maintaining special policies.
- The conflict threatens to damage the image of the organization or its employees who are not involved in the conflict.
- The unique nature of the conflict requires public exposure for the successful resolution.
- The unique nature of the conflict requires the organization to maintain jurisdiction over the conflict and be able to change the settlement of the conflict if the circumstances change.

Federal Mediation and Conciliation Service

The Administrative Dispute Resolution Act of 1996 amends Section 203 of the Labor Management Relations Act, 1947 (29 U.S.C. 173) by adding a statement that defines the role of Federal Mediation and Conciliation Service. The statement confirms that the Service is allowed to serve federal agencies as an adviser in the resolution of disputes. Such advice may be provided under the provisions of subchapter IV of chapter 5 of title 5, United States Code. The Act rules the following as the acceptable assistance:
- Aiding opposing parties in conflicts related to administrative programs
- Conducting training in alternative means of conflict resolution
- Equipping officers and employees of the Service to act as neutrals
- The ADR Act permits only officers and employees who are qualified in accordance with section 573 of title 5, United States Code, to act as neutrals.

ADR administrator duties

The duties of the ADR administrator are as follows:
- Select, train, and assign neutrals for various ADR options.
- Conduct mediation as a member of the Court's ADR Panel.
- Serve as liaison to judges, court clerk, and other staff.
- Direct and coordinate the ADR Program by providing strategic and master planning of ADR services.
- Coordinate revisions of the ADR Plan.
- Prepare the ADR budget.
- Collect and maintain biographical data on neutrals to ensure that assignments match the neutral's expertise.

Copyright © Mometrix Media. You have been licensed one copy of this document for personal use only. Any other reproduction or redistribution is strictly prohibited. All rights reserved.

- Make the neutrals' biographical data available to parties and counsel.
- Coordinate applications for funding and report on the utilization of funds.
- Maintain necessary documentation to administer and evaluate the options.
- Coordinate evaluation of the ADR Program.
- Maintain an active list of private or extra-judicial ADR providers.
- Monitor and present to judges, staff, lawyers, bench/bar groups and the public legal ADR developments in other courts and private ADR agencies.

Senior Counsel for Alternative Dispute Resolution

The Senior Counsel for Alternative Dispute Resolution within the Department of Justice has the following duties:

- Serve as an aid to senior management in developing ADR policies, including the Department Guidance on the Use of Alternative Dispute Resolution for Litigation in the Federal Courts
- Design and conduct ADR training
- Maintain records, assist in program evaluation and reporting
- Assist Department supervisors and employees with selecting cases for ADR and applying appropriate ADR techniques
- Report the status of the Department's ADR activities to the Attorney General
- Represent the Department in government-wide ADR activities
- Assist senior management with legislation, rulemaking, and policy creation
- Serve as the Dispute Resolution Specialist for the Department of Justice.

Arbitration

According to the Administrative Dispute Resolution Act of 1996, arbitration may be used as an alternative means of conflict resolution when the opposing parties agree to the following:

- Present only certain conflicts to arbitration
- Arbitration must make an award that is within a range of possible outcomes, and the maximum award must be specified
- None of the parties is required to agree to arbitration to enter into a contract or to obtain a benefit
- The parties have authority to enter into a settlement concerning the conflict
- The parties are authorized by the agency to agree to arbitration
- The head of an agency should consult the Attorney General and issue guidance before the parties enter into the binding arbitration.

Arbitrator

According to the Administrative Dispute Resolution Act of 1996 an arbitrator is a neutral who meets the following criteria:

- An individual who is a permanent or temporary Federal Government officer or employee, or any other individual whom the opposing parties consider acceptable.
- A neutral must not have any official, financial, or personal conflict of interest with the issues in controversy.
- If such interests exist, all parties must be notified of such interests and agree that the neutral may serve.
- The neutral must serve at the will of the conflicting parties.
- A neutral may be an employee of a professional agency specializing in conflict resolution.

Copyright © Mometrix Media. You have been licensed one copy of this document for personal use only. Any other reproduction or redistribution is strictly prohibited. All rights reserved.

- A neutral may be an employee of another professional agency that the first agency agrees to hire.

Arbitrator authorities

The following are the arbitrator's authorities as defined in The Administrative Dispute Resolution Act of 1996:

- Regulation of the course of arbitral hearings by setting the time and place of the hearing, notifying the parties, and preparing all the necessary components of the hearing
- Conducting arbitral hearings by interpreting and applying relevant regulations, laws, and policies
- Administrating oaths and affirmations ensuring proper recording
- Requiring and monitoring the attendance of witnesses during the hearing by employing such means of communication as telephone, television, computer, or other electronic means
- Requiring and monitoring production of oral or documentary evidence during the hearing with the privilege to exclude irrelevant, immaterial, or unduly repetitious evidence
- Making awards within 30 days after the hearing.

Arbitration proceedings

The following are the arbitration proceedings defined in the Administrative Dispute Resolution Act:

- Setting time and place for the hearing and notifying the parties at least 5 days ahead
- Preparation for the recording of the hearing on the part of the conflicting parties who prepare the copies and bear the costs of recording, and on the part of the

arbitrator who determines if the costs should be apportioned
- Conducting of the hearing, complete with presentation of the evidence and cross-examination of the witnesses
- Conducting of the hearing using electronic means if each party has an opportunity to participate
- Conducting of the hearing in a speedy and informal manner
- Receipt of the evidence and exclusion of any irrelevant, immaterial, or repetitious evidence
- Interpretation and application of regulations, laws, and policies
- Making an award within 30 days after the hearing, unless agreed otherwise.

Mandatory Mediation Settlement Conference

Mandatory Mediation Settlement Conference is a non-binding adjudication process where a neutral (such as a magistrate judge) works with the parties and their counsel at identifying issues, promoting a dialogue, and resolving the conflict. The main objective of this process is to assist the parties in proceeding to effective negotiation and resolution. Ten days before the conference, the parties must submit to the magistrate judge a joint copy of relevant pleadings and motions; a memorandum stating the legal and factual positions of parties in conflict; any other documents that each party views useful for the conference. All parties, or their representatives, and primarily responsible attorneys must be present at the conference. The magistrate judge should informally try to assist the parties in resolving all or some parts of the conflict. During the conference, the judge may hold separate, private discussions with any party or counsel, but may not

Copyright © Mometrix Media. You have been licensed one copy of this document for personal use only. Any other reproduction or redistribution is strictly prohibited. All rights reserved.

disclose the contents of the discussion to any other party or counsel. In case the parties have not arrived at the reasonable resolution of the conflict, the magistrate judge should propose a settlement that he/she considers reasonable. The magistrate judge concludes the conference when a settlement is reached or when further efforts are fruitless.

Mediator duties
- The mediator makes an opening statement explaining the process of mediation, the mediator's role, and the rules for the session.
- Each party provides an initial uninterrupted overview of the conflict.
- The mediator may hold a private meeting with each of the parties. The mediator may not disclose the communications which occurred during the meetings.
- The process of mediation may not be recorded or transcribed.
- The mediator assists the parties with identifying their interests and developing creative problem solving tactics for meeting those interests.
- The mediator determines the necessity of additional mediation sessions, and schedules the next session if necessary.
- Upon the completion, the mediator reports the results of the mediation session to the ADR Administrator.

Mediation in franchise law
In franchise law, the use of mediation for resolving contract execution conflicts is highly advantageous due to following reasons:
- Mediation is a non-binding means of ADR which allows the parties to continue their franchise relationship in the future.

- Mediation is cost effective and allows the parties to avoid the high monetary and other costs associated with formal conflict resolution procedures such as trials.
- Mediation allows the franchise partners to avoid the aggravations and hostility of litigation.
- Mediation is highly applicable to franchise conflicts.
- Mediation is very efficient since both parties intend to continue their franchise relationship.
- Mediation does not require discovery. Disclosure of communications is voluntary.
- Court-ordered mediation is applicable to franchise conflicts under the Federal Rules of Civil Procedure.

Summary jury/bench trial

Summary Jury/Bench Trial is a non-binding process where the parties present synopses of their cases to a mock jury or a judicial officer and use their decision to resolve the conflict. Before the trial, all materials pertaining to the case should be submitted. All parties, or their representatives, and their counsel must be present at the trial. Six jurors review the materials submitted and make their decision in a day or less. The Court may question members of a jury panel or determine whether to allow challenges. Each party makes a brief opening statement which may be recorded at the party's expense. The record may not be used as evidence in any subsequent trials. Counsels present a summary of the case, including opening statements, production of evidence, and final arguments. The judge gives the jury instructions, and the jury makes a decision. If the conflict is not resolved as the result of the jury's decision, it should proceed to full trial on the scheduled date.

Copyright © Mometrix Media. You have been licensed one copy of this document for personal use only. Any other reproduction or redistribution is strictly prohibited. All rights reserved.

Early Neutral Evaluation

Early Neutral Evaluation (ENE) is a pre-trial procedure where a neutral evaluator meets with the parties at the beginning of litigation process and assists them with organizing discovery, preparing the case for trial, and resolving of the conflict. The main role of the evaluator is to assess legal and factual aspects of the conflict and estimate the value of the case.

The duties of the neutral at the Early Neutral Evaluation procedure are as follows:
- Allow each party to make a brief oral statement outlining their position.
- Assist the parties with identifying areas of agreement and entering stipulations on the court record.
- Determine the parties' inclination to negotiate.
- Assist the parties with identifying issues that make up the conflict.
- Identify strengths and weaknesses of the parties' positions.
- Encourage the parties to make an agreement on an information exchange and discovery.
- Assist the parties with litigation cost assessment.
- Determine the necessity of additional conferences, schedule conferences, and assist with preparation of the necessary materials.
- Evaluate the parties' strengths and weaknesses and the probable outcome of the trial.
- Upon the completion, report the results of the evaluation to the ADR Administrator.

Conflict of interest

Any situation where an individual or a corporation is placed in a position in which they can abuse their professional capacity for their personal or corporate benefit may be defined as conflict of interest. It is also a situation where two or more parties in a position of trust have opposite or competing professional or personal interests. Clients, attorneys, and members of the investigative team may find themselves in conflict of interest which can make it impossible or very difficult for them to fulfill their duties impartially. Conflict of interest during an investigation may undermine the client's trust in the investigator or the investigator's trust in the client's good intentions. Conflict of interest is one of the reasons why the same law firm cannot represent both parties in a divorce case.

Attorney-client conflict of interest
Attorney-client relationships are protected by the Sixth Amendment which guarantees effective legal representation including the right of an accused to be represented by an attorney free of any conflicts of interest. In practice, it means that an attorney must not represent clients with adverse interests. For example, an attorney who has previously represented a client in a case must not represent another client in the same or closely related case. An attorney related to another attorney, as parent, child, sibling, or spouse, must not represent a client who is opposing the related attorney. An attorney related to the client as parent, child, sibling, or spouse, must not represent this client unless the client gives consent to do so.

Fiduciary duty and fiduciary conflict of interest
Fiduciary duty is a legal bond between two or more parties who are referred to as a "fiduciary" or "trustee" and a "principal" or "beneficiary". A fiduciary is expected to exercise absolute loyalty to the person he/she owes the duty (the "principal"). A fiduciary must put the duty before his/her personal interests and

- 12 -

Copyright © Mometrix Media. You have been licensed one copy of this document for personal use only. Any other reproduction or redistribution is strictly prohibited. All rights reserved.

must not gain pecuniary benefits from the fiduciary position. Any individual or corporation who manages financial assets or property for another and who must exercise a standard care imposed by law fulfills a fiduciary duty. A fiduciary conflict of interest is a situation where a fiduciary puts him/herself in a position where his/her personal or professional interests and fiduciary duty conflict.

Confidential and privileged communication

The following are the cases when the neutral may disclose confidential communication provided by the conflicting parties:

- All the parties have provided the written consent to disclose the communications.
- The communications have already been made public.
- The serious nature of the conflict requires the neutral to make the communications public if there is no other suitable person to disclose the communications.
- The court rules that disclosure of the communications is necessary to: a) prevent injustice; b) establish a violation of law; c) prevent significant damage to the public health or safety.
- The outcome of the confidential communications disclosure outweighs the importance of the conflict resolution proceedings integrity.

Rule of privileged communications
The rule of privileged communications is supported with the belief that certain communications must remain confidential. Only communications occurring within protected relationships are considered privileged. Protection of these relationships is viewed as more important than loss of evidence that could

result from the communications. The following rules must be observed while dealing with privileged communications:

- The assertion of the privileged can be done only by the holder of the privilege or an authorized representative of the holder.
- The privilege is waived if the holder fails to assert it after being presented with an opportunity to assert the privilege.
- The privilege is waived if the holder discloses all or part of communications to a party outside of the protected relationship.
- Communication must be directly related to the protected relationship to be considered privileged.
- Some of the privileged relationships are: attorney-client, husband-wife, physician-patient, accountant-client, priest-penitent, law enforcement-informant, reporter-source.

Husband-wife privilege
The communications between a husband and a wife which are made privately and are not intended for disclosure are protected by the privilege. A subject has a privilege to refuse to give testimony on any confidential communication which occurred between the subject and the spouse during their marriage. The subject also has a right to prevent another person from testifying on the confidential marital communications. The following cases are not covered by the privilege:

- If there is sufficient evidence that the spouses conspired or acted in cooperation in the crime charged.
- If the spouse is charged with a crime against the person or property of the other person, a minor, a child, or an individual residing in the household.

Copyright © Mometrix Media. You have been licensed one copy of this document for personal use only. Any other reproduction or redistribution is strictly prohibited. All rights reserved.

- In any case where the spouses are opposing parties.

Attorney-client privilege

The attorney-client privilege ensures confidentiality in legal matters. It covers all aspects of a case. Only the client may waive the privilege, agreeing to reveal information. It is the attorney's responsibility to inform the client that this privilege even exists. The privilege does not include non-lawyer personnel or prison lawyers. Both written and oral communication that occurred within the legal counsel is covered by this privilege. The privilege remains if the client had only the initial consultation and extends beyond the death of a client. Some of the aspects of attorney-client communications not covered by the privilege are the fee arrangement, physical evidence of a client's crime, information on future criminal activity. Also, in cases when the client files a malpractice lawsuit against the attorney, or when the attorney represents two clients who later become involved in a lawsuit against each other, communications are not covered by the privilege.

Accountant-client privilege

The accountant-client privilege, which is documented in the Internal Revenue Service Restructuring and Reform Act of 1998, guarantees confidentiality of communication between a client and his publicly certified accountant with respect to tax advice. The privilege may only be asserted in a non-criminal tax matter between the client and the IRS or in a non-criminal tax trial held in Federal Court between the client and the United States. The cases where the privilege does not cover the accountant-client communications include: any communications made before July 22, 1998; any written communication between a federally authorized tax

practitioner and a director, shareholder, officer, employee, agent, or representative of a corporation in connection with the promotion of the direct or indirect participation of such corporation in any tax shelter made before October 22, 2004.

Physician-patient privilege

The physician-patient privilege, which is based on the belief that any communication between doctor and patient is confidential, gives a physician the right to refuse to testify in a trial or other legal proceeding about any communication that occurred between the physician and the patient during the course of their protected relationship. A patient has the right to initiate litigation against the physician if the physician breaches the confidence in a testimony. In cases involving injuries, the physician has the plaintiff's permission to testify. When the defendant's physician conducts an examination of the injured plaintiff, he/she has to give permission for the examination and potential testimony in court. The privilege might not cover the physician-patient communications occurring between a psychiatrist and his/her patient, especially in criminal cases when the suspect confessed his/her crime in the communication with his/her psychiatrist.

Law enforcement-informant privilege

The law enforcement-informant privilege was first recognized in 1957, in the Roviaro v. United States case, 353 U.S. 53. The privilege guarantees protection to the federal law enforcement sources who share their knowledge to assist in the prosecution of criminal acts. Law enforcement agents have the privilege to refuse to disclose the identity of individuals who provided information. The following cases are exceptions to this rule:

- If the information was not found corroborative or reliable, the

Copyright © Mometrix Media. You have been licensed one copy of this document for personal use only. Any other reproduction or redistribution is strictly prohibited. All rights reserved.

informant's identity may have to be disclosed. The case may have to be dropped rather than have the informant testify in court. Unless there is a previous agreement regarding the court appearance, an informant should not ordinarily be required to appear in court.

- If the informant has done more than just provide information, and if it has been proven that he or she is a material witness whose testimony would be valuable.

Priest-penitent privilege

The priest-penitent privilege, or the clergy privilege, refers to the right to protect the contents of communications made between a member of the clergy and an individual who shares information with the intent not to be disclosed. The rules of the priest-penitent privilege are not as well defined as the other privilege rules. For example, in twenty-five states the priest-penitent privilege does not clearly state the holder; in seventeen states the penitent is stated as the holder of the privilege; in six states both a penitent and a priest are stated as the holders. The priest-penitent privilege may not cover communications in divorce, criminal, and ministerial misconduct cases. The privilege may also be waived in cases when the member of the clergy is a trained psychologist or secularly licensed counselor required by state law to report child abuse.

Reporter-source privilege

The reporter-source privilege is based on the First Amendment and gives a journalist the right to refuse to disclose identities of his/her sources of information. In many cases the privilege is the only rule that guarantees that the public will get access to classified information on the wrongdoing. In workplace investigations, the reporter-

source privilege is especially valid, since most employees might not agree to cooperate and share information in fear of retaliation on the part of the employer. In most states the limited reporter-source privilege is recognized. Under this limited privilege rule, a prosecutor can force disclosure of the source's identity if he/she can prove that there is no other way of obtaining the information.

Copyright © Mometrix Media. You have been licensed one copy of this document for personal use only. Any other reproduction or redistribution is strictly prohibited. All rights reserved.

Developing and Implementing Strategies

Case management

Case management is a formal mechanism that regulates planning and execution of any investigative operation, including collection and preservation of evidence, and communication with witnesses, victims, and suspects. Case management files serve as a case history. Any investigation requires case management in order to be successful. The following are the main purposes of case management:

- To record all the details pertaining to each stage of the investigation
- To serve as a reference for all the members of the current investigative team
- To maintain a chronological order of all the investigative operations
- To follow the progress of the investigation
- To serve as a reference for replacement or future investigators
- To serve as a basis for the client report in private investigations
- To present the case in court
- To present the case in the discovery process.

Activities and participants
Case management is executed through the following activities:
- Note taking – recording the facts observed at the crime scene, during surveillance, interviews and interrogations.
- Writing official reports – preparation of documents

containing a detailed account of each activity performed during the investigation; for example, interview report, surveillance report, and crime scene search report.
- Maintaining a folder containing all the documents, details, audio and video tapes, reports, and other information related to the investigation.

The following participate in case management activities:
- Primary investigator and other investigators – write reports, maintain chain of custody, and contribute to major information collection
- Case manager – administers the case, reviews reports, and communicates with other participants
- Witnesses – provide statements.

Case manager duties

Before the beginning of the investigation, the case manager should meet with the investigator and map out the goals and objectives of the investigation. Then the case manager should meet with the client to establish deadlines. After the meeting with the client, the case manager should make and disseminate the schedule of the investigative operations that match the client's deadlines. Then the case manager should oversee the investigator in developing an investigative plan. During the investigation, the case manager should schedule feedback sessions and provide support for the investigator. He/she should also collect regular investigative reports, usually weekly. In addition, the case manager should maintain files and records on each case in his/her custody. During the course of the investigation, the manager should document the investigator's performance at each stage.

Copyright © Mometrix Media. You have been licensed one copy of this document for personal use only. Any other reproduction or redistribution is strictly prohibited. All rights reserved.

Case Management File

Identification system

To make tracking and cross-referencing cases easier, a six-digit system is usually used to identify Case Management Files. The first two digits indicate the month when the file was established. The next two digits identify the sequential number of the case in that month. The last two digits indicate the year when the file was established. For example, the file number 06-01-06 means that the case file was established in June 2006, and it was the first case in that month. Larger investigative agencies may use letters to indicate the location of the branch where the file was established. For example, the file number 06-01-06-Cl-OH, means that the case file was established in June 2006, it was the first case in that month, and the file was established in Cleveland, Ohio.

Components

The following are the essential Case Management File (CMF) components:

- Incident or complaint form – contains name and contact information of the client or subject; date, time, location and description of the incident; names and contact information of individuals involved; and any other information pertaining to the incident.
- Witness interview statements with investigator summaries – contain written witness statements; CMF number, date and time of interview; investigator's name; and brief account of the interview.
- Results of records research form – contains sub-files on each interviewee, each type of record, and an index number for long records that cannot be stored in the CMF.

- Financial sub-file – contains all financial data related to the case.
- Surveillance report – contains all forms documenting surveillance conducted during the investigation.
- Case summary – documents the final results of the investigation and the disposition of the case; contains index data for future cross-reference.

Computerized case management systems

Computerized case management systems provide fast and efficient document and record management, as well as automated workflows. New case files are created with the help of pre-defined processes. The electronic case file structure corresponds to the appropriate official records retention system to ensure compliance with law. Web based systems provide a portal for sharing information and conducting collaborative searches within official records and document management repositories. An investigator receives a secure access to all the documents, records, communication, and business processes necessary for the progress of the investigation. All records and electronic evidence are securely preserved in compliance with law, the chain of custody and security requirements to be admissible in court.

Formalized case management procedures

Formalized case management procedures employed in federal law enforcement agencies require police officers to submit a Complaint Follow-Up report within three days of the receipt of the case. The first-line supervisor reviews the case with the investigator within seven days and determines if the case should be continued or closed. If the case is closed, a

Copyright © Mometrix Media. You have been licensed one copy of this document for personal use only. Any other reproduction or redistribution is strictly prohibited. All rights reserved.

recommendation for closing must be submitted. If the case is continued, the Case Folder must be established. The folder should contain the Complaint Follow-Up report, photographs, lab reports, rap sheets, index sheet for miscellaneous items, investigative plan, property clerk's invoice, court complaint forms, and investigative work sheets. The supervisor must review the case between the eighth and the twenty-first day and maintain the Individual Detective Case Log for each investigator assigned. Then, the supervisor establishes the Pattern Investigation Folder which is later maintained by the investigator assigned. The supervisor reviews the investigation again within thirty days and determines whether to close or continue the case.

Case assignment

There are several factors that influence each particular case assignment. Some of the factors are the organizational pattern of the investigative agency, crime classification, geographic location. Depending on the classification of the crime, the case may be forwarded directly to the specific investigator who is qualified to handle it. Otherwise, the complaint report may be directed first to the supervisor, who will make a decision about further case assignment based on the investigators' qualifications and workload. On average, an investigator receives one or two cases a day. Investigators who handle crimes against the property are assigned to more cases than investigators who handle crimes against the person. The supervisor usually determines if a specific case should be followed up by studying the potential options for solving and closing the case. Many cases are closed on the day of their receipt; only a few remain active for a few days.

Case evaluation

During the initial interview, the investigator should assess the quality and reliability of information and evaluate the case for integrity, credibility, and merit. The interview may reveal cases that are suspect and should be avoided. The following is a list of cases and clients that investigators should avoid if they can:

- Clients who inspire to change the world/society/community
- Crusaders
- Clients who are trying to avenge
- Clients who are trying to gain financial benefits
- Clients with emotional or mental disorders
- Clients who are trying to persuade the investigator in the merit of their case
- Clients who shop for professional services
- Clients who are trying to conceal their real motivation.

Client cost discussions

The following are guidelines on handling client cost discussions:

- Get some information on the client's business and financial history beforehand in order to estimate the client's financial status and protect yourself from potential denial of payment.
- During the first meeting don't hesitate to ask the client politely and tactfully to prove his/her financial stability.
- Analyze the proof provided and make a decision to undertake or decline the investigation.
- If your decision is positive, ask for additional information, such as bank data.
- Present and explain to the client all fees and expenses necessary to complete the investigation.

Copyright © Mometrix Media. You have been licensed one copy of this document for personal use only. Any other reproduction or redistribution is strictly prohibited. All rights reserved.

- Note the client's reaction and inclination to accept or negotiate the costs.
- Make the final decision.

Investigation strategy proposal

After the careful evaluation of the case based on the criteria of time, resources, meaningful objectives, and evidence of law breach, the case manager should prepare an investigation strategy proposal to be presented to the client. The proposal should contain the following elements:

- Executive summary of the proposal
- Analysis of the purpose and scope of the investigation
- Detailed objectives
- Recommendations on how to achieve objectives
- Technical details related to the recommendations
- An estimate of costs
- Anticipated results and timeline
- Response to anticipated client's questions
- Details on licensing and insurance
- Professional qualifications of all investigative staff who will be involved
- Professional references.

Elements to analyze before the investigation

The success of the investigation depends on the case manager's ability to correctly estimate time, cost, resource allocation, and solvability of the case. The following elements must be analyzed prior to engaging in an investigation:

- Management commitment – preparedness to dedicate time and invest sufficient funds.
- Investment of time – the incident's scope, the investigator's

experience, and objectives of the investigation determine its length.

- Resources – the case manager must assess how much time is necessary for each step of the investigation, what expenses can be expected during each activity, what kind of personnel is required to perform the tasks.
- Meaningful objectives – the client should clearly state the meaningful objectives of the investigation, otherwise the operation is not worthwhile.
- Evidence of policy violation or serious misconduct – the case manager should be familiar with laws and policies well enough to determine if there is a valid reason for investigation.

Competent investigations

Each competent investigation should have the following five traits:

- Objectivity – the facts collected and interpreted during the investigation must be presented in an objective manner without any biases or influences of the investigator's experience and knowledge.
- Thoroughness – information collected during the investigation must be verified several times using diverse sources to ensure relevancy, accuracy, and currency.
- Relevance – information collected during the investigation should be relevant to the case. The investigator should check relevance of any information several times before deciding to accept or discard that information.
- Accuracy – information collected during the investigation should be as accurate as possible. The investigator should filter through

Copyright © Mometrix Media. You have been licensed one copy of this document for personal use only. Any other reproduction or redistribution is strictly prohibited. All rights reserved.

witnesses' statements and other information to obtain an exact description or account of events.

- Currency – facts and evidence collected in the course of the investigation should be as up-to-date as possible to ensure relevance and accuracy.

Investigative resources

Investigative resources can be defined as any human, material, and financial resources necessary to successfully start, progress, and complete an investigation. Human resources include investigators, surveillants and their aides, case managers, subject matter experts, secretaries and communication specialists, and other personnel directly or indirectly involved in the investigation. Material resources include surveillance equipment, such as video and photo cameras, audio recorders, vehicles, computers and software; crime scene processing equipment, such as containers, chemical substances, etc.; interview and interrogation equipment, such as office space, audio recorder, etc. Financial resources include any monetary funds necessary for continuing the investigation. Financial resources may be cash for vehicle fuel, payment for long-distance phone calls, and compensation to informants.

Investigation plan

The following are the essential components of an investigation plan:

- Preparation – the first stage of the investigation, at which the type of the investigation is determined, investigative methods are chosen, cost-benefit analysis is conducted, personnel are selected, and resources are allocated.
- Learning – the next stage of the investigation, at which collection

of information occurs by means of research, interviewing, and evidence gathering.

- Analysis – the most important stage of the investigation, at which the collected data is interpreted, and conclusions and recommendations are made.
- Notification – the final stage of the investigation, at which the investigator informs the client about the completion of the investigation and its results.

Preparation phase

The preparation phase of the investigation begins with determining the type of the investigation, such as employment background inquiry, financial frauds, loss prevention, sexual harassment, computer crime, employee theft, violence in the workplace, drug and alcohol abuse, arson, larceny, traffic accidents, battery and assault, or relationship investigations. As soon as the type is determined it is necessary to select the investigative methods. For example, for larceny, arson, and traffic accidents, crime scene processing and lab analysis of the evidence are the primary methods. For employment background inquiries, research is the essential method. For financial frauds, loss prevention, and relationship investigations, surveillance is the most fruitful method. After the selection of the methods, human, material, and financial investigative resources should be allocated.

Investigative resource allocation
Based on the cost-benefit analysis the primary investigator makes a decision on how to allocate resources. The allocation of resources largely depends on the type of the investigation at hand. For example, in workplace cases where multiple employees are skimming funds, it is necessary to conduct surveillance of each

Copyright © Mometrix Media. You have been licensed one copy of this document for personal use only. Any other reproduction or redistribution is strictly prohibited. All rights reserved.

employee to expose them. Therefore, a large portion of the resources will be dedicated to surveillance and documentation of its results. If surveillance equipment is going to be used, significant funds should be spent on the state-of-the-art technology, its maintenance, and staff training. Computer crime investigations usually demand the use of highly experienced personnel or third-party experts. Therefore, the resources will be dedicated to compensating experts for their services. If the investigation is concerned with exposing fraudulent behavior in a casino, large amounts of cash will be needed to obtain information in this setting.

Analysis phase
The analysis phase of the investigation is the most important as this is the stage where the conclusion is reached and recommendations are made. At this stage, all the information collected during the learning phase is analyzed and interpreted in relation to the investigation. Therefore, it is important for the investigator to have strong reasoning skills. Usually, two types of reasoning are used for analysis: inductive reasoning and deductive reasoning. The value of the inductive analysis is measured through plausibility and truth of the argument based on the results of the interpretation of evidence and information. The value of the deductive analysis is measured through validity and truth of the argument. The analysis phase of the investigation is completed with thorough examination of the reasoning behind the conclusions.

Inductive reasoning
Induction or inductive reasoning is the process of reasoning where the premises of an argument support the conclusion but do not guarantee it. Inductive reasoning involves observing concrete characteristics while drawing general conclusions. Induction uses limited

observations or experiences to ascribe general properties and relations or to establish laws. For example, it is known that a suspect of workplace theft did not open the facility with the employee key. It is also known that all employees have keys to the facility. Therefore, the conclusion is that the suspect must not be an employee. However, the suspect might not have used the key in order not to be traced. The value of inductive reasoning is measured by plausibility and truth. Plausibility can be assessed by applying the conclusion to a number of individual cases. Truth is assessed by measuring the correctness of premises and conclusions.

Deductive reasoning
Deduction, or deductive reasoning draws the conclusion, which is as specific as the premises. The conclusion cannot be true while the premises are false. Deduction uses general rules and laws to interpret new specific examples. In deductive reasoning, the same general law can be applied to an indefinite number of new pieces of information. For example, all employees at the X Corporation have a PAD key to the inventory area. Tom is an employee of the X Corporation, therefore he has a PAD key to the inventory area. The value of the deductive reasoning may be measured through validity and truth. Validity stands for logical correctness of the argument. The argument is considered valid if both the premise and the conclusion are logically correct. Truth is assessed by examining separately the correctness of the premise and the conclusion.

Learning phase
At the learning stage, the investigator should collect as much information related to the case as possible. First, it is necessary to familiarize oneself with the matter of the investigation. This can be done by conducting research, consulting subject matter experts, or employing staff that possess knowledge of the subject of

Copyright © Mometrix Media. You have been licensed one copy of this document for personal use only. Any other reproduction or redistribution is strictly prohibited. All rights reserved.

the investigation. The primary investigator should recognize staff members who can be of assistance by either sharing their knowledge or deepening it while conducting research. Data obtained with the help of subject matter experts should be filtered and presented objectively in order to avoid bias and ensure accuracy and relevance of information. The investigator should compile a list of bibliographical references to keep track of all the sources.

Notification phase

Notification is the last phase of the investigation. It completes the investigation by presenting the final report of the case to the client or supervisor. The report should begin with an executive summary briefly stating what is going to be discussed in the report. Dissemination of the report should be done through confidential channels, such as secure delivery or internal e-mail communication. If there are multiple recipients of the report, the document should be accompanied with the security instructions, which explain how to handle the report when it is not in control of its recipient. If litigation is recommended as a method of conflict resolution, the report might be requested during the discovery.

Efficient time management

The following are the investigative practices that ensure efficient time management:

- Reducing time in briefing and assigning investigators by doing it in groups in pre-assigned time.
- Keeping the telephone conversations short and to the point.
- Using automated systems for report editing, appointment scheduling, and customer correspondence.

- Reducing the time in meetings with management, supervisors, and other investigators by eliminating long pointless discussions.
- Planning all the daily activities ahead of time.
- Assigning administrative staff to handle dictated correspondence, journals, etc.
- Coordinating assignments of handling officials to investigators.
- Using consolidated reports instead of multiple individual reports.
- Reducing length of Schedule of Investigative Services by eliminating redundancy and unnecessary information.

Scheduling techniques

Since many of investigators are involved in several cases or are performing several roles simultaneously, it is very important for them not to get confused in the scheduling process and to avoid conflicting interview appointments. Before planning any appointments, the investigator should have some idea of the depth and breadth of an interview in order to estimate the time required to complete the appointment. It should be noted that first time visits usually take longer than subsequent visits. To ensure that the interviews do not go over the allocated time, reminder cards could be sent to interviewees indicating the time and date of the appointment. For a large amount of appointments, a scheduler folder or a computer schedule system could be used to facilitate efficient and organized operation.

Note taking

As soon as important information related to the investigation is obtained, a report documenting every detail of this

Copyright © Mometrix Media. You have been licensed one copy of this document for personal use only. Any other reproduction or redistribution is strictly prohibited. All rights reserved.

information must be written. Each investigator should have a notebook of his/her own in order to document information in synchronous manner. All notes in the notebook should be numbered in chronological order. Pages in the notebook should be numbered in order to keep track of information. The first page should contain the name of the investigator, the date and time when the notebook was opened and closed, the name of the agency to which the investigator belongs, and the case name and number. Notes should be as descriptive as possible to assist the investigator in writing a report later. Audio recording devices should not replace note taking. A completed notebook should be kept for future reference.

Recording tasks and costs

Fees and expenses should be recorded and kept track of in fact sheets, such as Preliminary Fact Sheet and Ongoing Fact Sheet. All costs should be entered beforehand in order to estimate the total and notify the client of the anticipated expenditures. The Preliminary Fact sheets should contain the following:

- A list of tasks to consider, such as initial client and witness interviews, preparation of memos, review and analysis of public documents
- Start and end date
- Hours
- Costs to consider, such as copying, document processing, research, investigator fees, and travel.

The Ongoing Fact sheets should contain the same information, although the list of tasks to consider is different. For example, follow-up client and witness interviews, review client documentation, review, analysis, and organization of public documents.

Time and expense report

To keep track of the time spent on billable tasks, the following should be included in the time and expense report:

- Client's name, address, and phone number – serves as client identification.
- Title of the operation performed – indicates the billable task.
- Billing office area number and client number – serves as client billing identification.
- Issuing office area number – serves as investigator billing identification.
- Description, date, time, hours, and rate of services provided – show the client that the time and money were spent on the tasks related to the investigation.
- Local and business fares – shows local expenses.
- Telephone, auto, meals, and lodging expenses – should be supported with receipts.
- An itemized list of other expenses – should also be supported with receipts.
- Calculated grand total – shows the sum of all expenses.
- Name and signature of the handling official – serves as confirmation.

Inappropriate employment application questions

The following questions are considered inappropriate in employment applications according to state and federal laws:

- Request to disclose the original name of the applicant whose name has been changed
- Request to provide the birthplace of the applicant's family who resides outside of the US

Copyright © Mometrix Media. You have been licensed one copy of this document for personal use only. Any other reproduction or redistribution is strictly prohibited. All rights reserved.

- Request to present military discharge documents
- Inquiry into foreign military service
- Requirement to indicate the applicant's race
- Requirement to provide a photo
- Request to disclose the applicant's membership in race, nationality, and religion based organizations
- Request to provide address of the applicant's parents and family members
- Inquiry into the citizenship of the applicant's spouse or parents
- Request to disclose the applicant's religion
- Request to disclose age when it is not related to the occupational qualifications or federal and state minimum age laws.

Pre-employment investigations

Pre-employment investigations are investigations initiated by the employer in order to determine the job applicant's suitability for the position. Pre-employment investigations are conducted before the employer makes a job offer and are aimed at checking the applicant's background. The following are the investigative methods used in pre-employment investigations:
- Checking the applicant's criminal history in order to predict potential problems
- Reviewing the applicant's educational background, such as schools attended, degrees obtained, training received, dates, etc. to determine if the applicant is qualified for the position
- Checking the applicant's financial status, such as credit history, bankruptcy, repossession, etc.
- Interviewing references about the applicant's reputation

- Checking medical records for history of mental or emotional disorders
- Reviewing social affiliations in order to prevent potential conflicts.

Computer crime

Computer crime can be defined as any illegal act that involves the use of a computer in either of the three classifications: 1) as the object of the crime; 2) as an instrument with which the crime was committed; 3) as the evidence storage device. Any traditional crime, such as theft, fraud, forgery, sexual harassment, etc. can be committed with the help of a computer and thus be classified as a computer crime. Computer misuse of abuse are not considered crimes if the intent of the user did not result in violation of the law. The following are types of computer crime: 1) fraud by manipulation; 2) forgery; 3) damage or modification; 4) unauthorized access; 5) unauthorized reproduction.

<u>Computer forgery</u>
Computer forgery is a crime that involves alteration of data on electronically stored documents. Cases of computer forgery include falsification of identification documents, for instance driver's licenses, resident cards, passports, visas; financial documents, such as checks, loans, invoices, bank statements, credit card statements; and property papers, for example titles, ownership documents, mortgages. Modern computer software and hardware allows even an amateur to copy, modify, create, and produce almost any document. The quality of the forged documents may vary depending on the equipment used and the level of protection on the original. Some of the falsified copies are very hard to detect, while others can be spotted by an untrained individual.

Copyright © Mometrix Media. You have been licensed one copy of this document for personal use only. Any other reproduction or redistribution is strictly prohibited. All rights reserved.

Computer fraud manipulation

Computer fraud by manipulation involves fraudulent transaction of intangible assets existing in the form of data. Computer fraud by manipulation may involve the use of personal and financial data, for example credit cards for unauthorized transactions. There are several types of manipulation: input manipulation, program manipulation, and output manipulation. Input manipulation involves entering faulty data in order to receive financial or other gain. Input manipulation crimes are the easiest to commit and the most difficult to detect. Program manipulation involves tampering with the computer software in order to receive financial or other gain. Program manipulation crimes require expert knowledge of computer programming. This type of crime is more difficult to commit, but also difficult to detect. Output manipulation involves falsification of the initial instructions in order to produce a specific output result, such as increasing the amount of cash dispensed by the ATM machine.

Computer unauthorized access

Unauthorized access, which can be gained with the help of a "Trojan Horse" program, can be used to cause damage to the system, to crash networks, to eliminate files, to block authorized users, to steal information, or to modify data. In most cases, unauthorized access is gained remotely, so that it is harder to trace the attempt. Username and password login systems are designed to counteract unauthorized access perpetrators; however, experienced perpetrators have the ability to "crack" even the most complicated password protection systems. The code cracking programs are easily available from many computer expert websites and are regularly updated with the most sophisticated versions. Unauthorized interception of telecommunications, such as emails, phone conversations, etc. is also classified as a computer unauthorized access crime. The most common motive for this crime is obtaining free services or disguising criminal activity.

Computer damage or modification

Computer damage or modification, also sabotage, involves creation and dissemination of destructive computer programs, commonly known as "Trojan horse," "virus," and "worm." A computer virus is an executable program that attaches itself to a program or file and spreads from one computer to another, leaving infections. To spread the virus, it is necessary to share the infected files or programs by sending them in an email or through the network. A worm has the ability to replicate itself and travel unaided through file or information transport features on the system. "Trojan Horse" appears to be useful software but does damage; for example, it gives unauthorized users access to the system. Destructive computer programs can be targeted at inhibition of network systems, modification, or elimination of data. Computer sabotage is used to eliminate competitors, gain financial benefits, or in terrorist activity.

Computer unauthorized reproduction

Unauthorized reproduction can be defined as a criminal act which involves illegal copy, production, and dissemination for financial profit of the whole or part of electronic products, such as software, music and video CDs, and DVDs. Unauthorized reproduction causes significant economic losses to the authoring manufacturers of the product while giving perpetrators a chance to gain quick profits. In some Asian and Eastern European countries unauthorized reproduction laws are more lenient than in North America, therefore most of the unauthorized reproduction crimes occur overseas, where they are more difficult to detect and prosecute. The unauthorized reproduction laws in North America are

Copyright © Mometrix Media. You have been licensed one copy of this document for personal use only. Any other reproduction or redistribution is strictly prohibited. All rights reserved.

being developed and there are more precedents every year, so it is easier to detect the unauthorized reproduction crime and prosecute the perpetrators living and operating in North America.

Computer crime investigation

Procedures
The procedures in computer investigations are as follows:
- Prepare virus protection software capable of detecting and eliminating malicious programs, and repairing infected or damaged files.
- Prepare storage disks, markers and tags to mark the recovered information.
- Make sure that none of the employees have access to computer equipment linked to the system under investigation.
- Identify and document types of computer equipment and software involved.
- Make sure the modems are disconnected.
- Obtain usernames and passwords.
- Identify and document backup procedures.
- Photograph the system to prove its operational condition.
- Search for clues, such as manuals or discarded software packs in the area surrounding the computer equipment.
- Record each step in the investigation, back up any recovered data, and store the data as evidence according to the standard evidence preservation procedures.

Methods
Methods employed in computer crime investigations, which are a combination of traditional investigative methods and high-tech methods, include the following:

- Computer search – determine if the computer is the tool or the object of the crime; delete sensitive data if necessary; install a booby trap to detect an unauthorized access; determine the need to keep the system in operation; search access controlled systems; use password identification software programs.
- Media search – search for hidden files and invisible disk space; read graphic files and convert them into raster; search electronic communication, such as e-mail, saved IMS messages, etc.; create a bitstream image of the system.
- External inspection – search the area where the computer is located, paying attention to unmarked disks, printouts, and peripheral devices, such as routers, printer servers, repeaters, etc.

Preparation
Before starting a computer crime investigation, it is necessary to conduct a computer search. However, it is important to know all the details about the computer system itself in order to conduct an efficient search. Therefore, the investigator should collect as much information as possible about the computer system. The following data is required:
- System configuration – stand-alone, LAN, WAN, dial-up connection, other connection
- Type of hardware – CPU
- Storage capacity, memory capacity
- Types, versions, and brands of installed software
- Type of modem, speed, bandwidth
- Security systems – password protection, encryption, access control

Copyright © Mometrix Media. You have been licensed one copy of this document for personal use only. Any other reproduction or redistribution is strictly prohibited. All rights reserved.

- Presence of booby traps – programs that delete information if an unauthorized access has been detected
- Physical location of the system.

Federal criminal statutes concerning financial crime

The following are federal criminal statutes concerning financial crime:
- 18 U.S.C. 215 – prohibits corruption and bribery, makes it illegal for officers, directors, employees, agents, or attorneys of financial institutions to solicit, demand or accept anything of value from any person.
- 18 U.S.C. 641 – prohibits embezzlement, stealing, purloin, or any other unauthorized use of public funds, property, or records.
- 18 U.S.C. 656 – prohibits embezzlement, theft, or misapplication by bank officer or employee.
- 18 U.S.C. 1344 – prohibits financial institution frauds.
- 18 U.S.C. 1001 – prohibits knowingly making general falsified statements.
- 18 U.S.C. 1005 – prohibits officers and employees of financial institutions from making false entries, including material omissions.
- 18 U.S.C. 1014 – prohibits fraudulent loan and credit applications, renewals and discounts, crop insurance.
- 18 U.S.C. 1341 and 1343 – prohibit fraud by mail, wire, radio, or television.
- 18 U.S.C. 2 and 371 – prohibit general offences and frauds.

Workplace theft and fraud

Prevention
The following are the most common methods for effective workplace fraud and theft prevention:
- Reduce the number of motivated offenders by publishing names of apprehended fraudsters and thieves, including detailed descriptions of sanctions taken against them.
- Recognize employees who may potentially engage in fraudulent behavior by screening the employees for attitude, company loyalty, and job satisfaction.
- Monitor daily operation patterns, unusual activity, and customer concerns/complaints.
- Educate employees about the possibility of a judicial punishment.
- Protect and educate targets of fraud and theft (employees and customers) by disseminating information about potential frauds.
- Limit opportunities for fraud and theft by fortifying the company's policies and regulations and re-enforcing punitive measures.

Clark and Hollinger's studies of workplace show that the most influential factors in employee theft deterrence are the following: 1) perceived certainty; 2) perceived severity; 3) age; 4) gender. Perceived certainty is a level of risk of punishment or apprehension the deviant employee expects in response to his/her acts. If the employee is aware of the imminent punishment from management, peers, or third party investigators, he or she is less likely to engage in theft. Perceived severity is the level of punishment following the act of larceny. The sanctions against a deviant employee in an organizational setting might include

Copyright © Mometrix Media. You have been licensed one copy of this document for personal use only. Any other reproduction or redistribution is strictly prohibited. All rights reserved.

peer ostracism, management reprimand, dismissal, and, ultimately, police notification. Age is not marked as a substantial factor in workplace theft deterrence, however, it has been noted that employees under 25 tend to underestimate the risk of apprehension and punishment. Gender is a significant factor in larceny deterrence as females are less likely to be involved in deviant acts, especially after a verbal sanction. Males are more willing to take higher punishment risks.

Fraudulent behavior

According to Donald Cressey's theory, the following elements must be present in an organization for its employees to be potentially involved in frauds:

- Pressures/incentives to commit fraud
- Opportunity and shared responsibility
- Rationalization.

The pressures or incentives can be characterized as factors influencing employees' decisions to engage in fraudulent behavior. These factors can range from low wages to dissatisfaction with the organization and frustration at bureaucracy. The opportunity for fraud arises when organizations practice shared responsibility policies. Duties become redistributed among fewer employees, therefore the overall level of responsibility decreases causing the employees to engage in fraudulent behavior. Rationalization can be defined as justification of fraud based on the imitation of the attitude of the top officials in the organization. If the high ranking employees display disregard of ethics, policies, and regulations, other employees see it as a rationale to justify their own deviant behavior.

Lapping fraud

"Lapping" is known as one of the concealment techniques employees use to skim funds from accounts receivable. It involves crediting of one account with the money taken from another account. The "lapping" scheme can be described as follows: The employee skims money from Customer A's account; to cover the shortage of balance in Customer A's account, Customer B's funds are used. The scheme continues endlessly until it is discovered in one of the following ways:

- One of the accounts is compensated
- A concealing entry is made to adjust the account balance.

Since the scheme is complicated, employees participating in "lapping" keep a separate set of records to track the actual payments.

Small business skimming frauds

The following are the most typical skimming frauds that employees in small business can commit:

- Unrecorded sales – the employee takes the cash funds from a customer without recording the sale.
- False transaction – the employee rings the "no sale" transaction while taking the cash.
- Off-hour sales – the employee performs sales outside of normal business hours without recording the sales in the company's books.
- Mail-Room Theft – the mail-room employees in charge of opening mail take the incoming checks without recording the receipt of the funds.
- Check-For-Cash Substitution – the employee takes the cash funds from the daily operations and substitutes them with a rebate or refund check which was received earlier and not recorded.
- Inventory Shrinkage – the employee takes the cash from the customer and then removes the

Copyright © Mometrix Media. You have been licensed one copy of this document for personal use only. Any other reproduction or redistribution is strictly prohibited. All rights reserved.

purchased item from the inventory to conceal the fraud.

Phantom employee fraud investigation

The following steps are recommended in phantom employee fraud investigation:

- Start with examining personnel files focusing on social security numbers and W-2 tax forms.
- Verify the social security number in question.
- Compare the employee and payroll lists.
- Examine and compare payroll amounts with recorded salaries.
- Inspect travel expense documents, bonuses, other documents that may reveal exaggerated amounts.
- Examine the paycheck and determine if it was cashed or deposited.
- Identify the person who endorsed the check.
- Obtain and examine account statements.
- Examine other payment methods, such as money orders, wire transfers, withdrawal, traveler's checks, cashier's checks, etc.
- Trace the movements of the check from the issuance to deposit.

Cost/benefit analysis in employee theft

While analyzing costs and benefits of taking action and remaining passive in employee theft, the following areas must be considered:

- Psychological
- Social
- Financial

The cost of remaining passive may be reflected in these areas in the following ways:

- Psychological – undermining authority
- Social – damage of employees' status, negative impact on discipline, marring of the company's reputation

- Financial – creation of a precedent for potential crimes, acceptance of loss, actual loss due to criminal activity.

The cost of taking an action may be reflected in these areas in the following ways:

- Psychological – embarrassment of the organization, emotional reaction of employees
- Social – too much control can cause disgruntlement
- Financial – loss of clientele due to negative publicity, additional expenses on replacements, human resources, and legal fees.

Undercover employee theft investigations

The most common tactics of undercover employee theft investigation include:

- The wedge – the operative's visible engagement in other criminal activity or misconduct, such as alcohol or drug abuse, in order to gain trust of the alleged perpetrators.
- Use of third parties – another investigator whose identity must be kept secret for a while may pose as an associate engaged in criminal activity; this creates an effect of suspense and also helps build trust.
- Selling small items for heavily discounted prices – this makes the operative look like a low-level fence with possible ties in criminal circles by implying but never admitting that the goods are stolen.
- Buy-bust operation – arresting the perpetrator while he/she is selling or buying stolen goods;
- Sting operation – similar to buy-bust, but involves a more complicated setup, such as establishing a cover business or

Copyright © Mometrix Media. You have been licensed one copy of this document for personal use only. Any other reproduction or redistribution is strictly prohibited. All rights reserved.

store front where the stolen goods are sold and bought.

The following are the steps in undercover employee theft investigation:
- Selection of an operative
- Placement of the selected operative
- Planning of tactics

The success of the operation largely relies on the selection of an operative; therefore this step is the most important. The choice of an operative depends on the type of theft, as specific theft experience is required of an operative. Physical experience as well as emotional preparation is expected of an expert undercover theft operative. The placement of the operative follows the selection and should be conducted discretely using a cold or controlled hire. The cover position should be planned beforehand and allow the operative as much mobility and exposure to the area where the goods are being stolen as possible. The planning of tactics step follows the placement of the operative and requires knowledge of the ongoing criminal activity. The theft type determines tactics.

Areas to search
The following areas should be searched for signs of employee theft:
- Employee lockers – may reveal signs of substance abuse, gambling, or theft.
- Work areas – desks, filing cabinets, and boxes should be searched for the signs of falsified documents and altered records.
- Secured areas – security rooms and cages should be inspected as they are suitable areas to hide signs of theft.
- Restrooms – toilet tanks, ventilation ducts, waste baskets, plumbing access doors, and shelves should be examined for

wrapping materials of stolen items and signs of substance abuse.
- Full case areas – warehouse areas where full cases are kept; should be checked for fullness.
- Concealed and hard to reach areas – stairwells, elevator pits, roofs, ventilation ducts, and other concealed places should be examined for signs of theft.

Investigation methods
An employee theft investigation starts with the inventory check, both record and physical. Significant losses discovered during this step may indicate theft, internal or external. The next step is to identify the weak spots in the inventory system, such as double counts, absence or presence of an auditor, weaknesses of the computerized inventory system, etc. It is also important to check the records of opening and closing and consult with the alarm company to find out if the facilities have been opened outside the regular business hours. Some of the other most common methods are surprise cash counts, inspection of cash register irregularities, proper sales documentation, and checking for returns without purchase. The next step is to search the workplace for clues of the theft that would point to a suspect.

Prevention
The steps to prevent employee theft include the following:
- Conducting pre-employment background checks to determine if the applicant has a criminal history, has undergone disciplinary or correction actions, is a job-hopper, or has certain traits of character that may indicate his/her tendency to steal
- Devising and implementing workplace policies which clearly define theft and disciplinary

Copyright © Mometrix Media. You have been licensed one copy of this document for personal use only. Any other reproduction or redistribution is strictly prohibited. All rights reserved.

measures against employees who engage in this criminal activity

- Creating a working environment based on loyalty and trust between co-workers and management
- Discussing employee theft case studies during regular meetings
- Detecting and mediating workplace conflicts, especially conflicts between workers and management
- Ensuring that management has proper qualifications for supervision and control of employees
- Investing in high-security systems.

Cargo theft

Investigation techniques
The following techniques are used in cargo theft investigations:

- Use of informants – individuals who come from a cargo related background and have motivation to assist with the investigation.
- Undercover investigation – demands specific knowledge of cargo handling, suitable physical appearance.
- Surveillance – includes air, vessel, and hardware methods.
- Use of technical equipment – electronic sensors, fluorescent powders, photography, infrared and night vision devices, videotaping and closed circuit television.
- Telephone number analysis – review of phone call patterns.
- Identification of "fence" operations – detection of points of receipt and distribution of stolen goods.
- Identification of cargo documentation forgery – detection of manipulation with

the documents accompanying cargo. Requires specific knowledge of cargo importation and movement papers.

Pilferage
Pilferage is a crime of theft of small items, usually from shipping packages. Pilferage may occur during cargo shipment. One of the methods of preventing cargo shipment pilferage is to apply a seal. The seal must be affixed at the point of origin, i.e. at the point of loading, by an authorized representative of the loading company immediately after the loading is completed. The loading company must provide proof of seal application by recording the seal number, location, date and time of installation in the Bill of Lading, Ship's Manifest or CCD (Cargo Control Document). The receiver of the shipment must verify the seal number and establish its integrity upon the delivery of the cargo.

Cargo theft report
The following information must be included in the cargo theft report:

- Name of the vessel, aircraft, or vehicle
- Date and time conveyance should arrive
- Foreign port of lading, in case of import
- Bill of lading number or airway bill number
- Foreign shipper and manufacturer identification
- Customs broker identification, if applicable
- Name of ultimate consignee
- Serial numbers, tags, or other identification marks on stolen items
- Retail value of stolen items
- Status of stolen items, imported or exported
- Name of the individual who discovered theft

Copyright © Mometrix Media. You have been licensed one copy of this document for personal use only. Any other reproduction or redistribution is strictly prohibited. All rights reserved.

- Location, date, and time of theft
- Date and time the theft was reported to the authorities
- Identification of the authority to which the theft was reported.

Marine cargo movement procedures

These procedures must be followed before the pickup:

- The steamship company receives a copy of the vessel's cargo manifest. The consignee is notified two days before the arrival of the vessel. Freight release is facilitated by the carrier.
- The Customs broker or consignee obtains freight release and Department of Agriculture clearance prior to contacting the motor carrier. The motor carrier receives the bill of lading and an authorization to pick up the cargo.
- The motor carrier makes an agreement with the steamship company about the time during which the cargo may be picked up and appropriate transportation containers. The driver receives a copy and the original of the pickup order and departs for the pier to be in time for an appointment with the terminal operator made 24 hours in advance.

These procedures must be followed during the pickup:

- The driver obtains a customs cartman identification card. If the cargo is transported by common or private carriers, the card is not required.
- The driver is issued a pass at the gate house. The terminal operator checks the pickup order and directs the driver to the pier Customs office.
- The Customs inspector verifies the pickup order, the

identification card, and other papers against the Customs entry documents. If all the requirements are met, the inspector authorizes the pick up order with the "Delivery Authorized" stamp.

- The terminal operator directs the driver to the loading area and the shipment is loaded by the pier personnel. At this time, the checker must document any shortages and report them to the Customs inspector in the form of joint determination. The terminal operator retains the original pickup order.

Air cargo movement procedures

These procedures must be followed for air cargo movement:

- The aircraft arrives at the port and obtains clearance from the Public Health Department.
- The cargo is unloaded by the port personnel.
- The airline verifies the completeness of the cargo against the air bill and notifies the consignee.
- The Customs broker or the consignee prepares the entry and sends the air bill and the pickup order to the inland carrier.
- The Customs officer authorizes the delivery after examination of all the accompanying documents. A portion of the shipment may be designated for an appraisal.
- The motor carrier presents the pickup order to the terminal operator and obtains the authorization to load the shipment.
- For inbound cargo, the motor carrier and the airline representatives make a joint determination and submit it to the Customs officer.

Copyright © Mometrix Media. You have been licensed one copy of this document for personal use only. Any other reproduction or redistribution is strictly prohibited. All rights reserved.

Property pass

A property pass is a legal document permitting employees to remove the company's property for various purposes. The property pass is issued by authorized personnel and can be valid for up to a year. Only employees responsible for certain items of property can be issued a property pass. The reasons for issuing a property pass might be as follows:

- Relocation of property, for example equipment for repair or maintenance
- Removal of property due to temporary assignment of an employee using the property to a different location, for example telecommuting
- Any other removal of property due to the internal company movements and operations.

The security personnel are notified that the item is authorized for removal and record the item of property's new temporary location.

Undercover workplace investigations

Common mistakes
The following are the common mistakes made in undercover workplace investigations:

- Absence of clear objectives – a result of the client's inability to articulate the specific objectives of an undercover investigation. To avoid this mistake, the investigator should obtain a comprehensive needs list which can be used to determine measurable objectives.
- Poor planning and lack of attention to details – complexity of many investigations prevents the investigators from devising a clear step-by-step plan that takes into account as many details as possible. To avoid this, the

investigator should allocate sufficient time for appropriate planning before starting the investigation.
- Overstaffing – complexity of investigations may cause the investigators to employ more people than necessary. To avoid this, the investigator must understand that overstaffing slows and increases the cost of the investigation.

Preparation
To ensure that the undercover workplace investigation is effective and does not interfere with the routine operations of the company, the following preparation steps must be taken:

- No signs of questionable or improper activity must be visible.
- Employees should not be distracted from their everyday duties.
- Investigative communication must be restricted to no more than three participants, excluding counsel.
- Investigative communication must remain confidential even after the investigation is completed.
- No actions that would alert the alleged perpetrator must be taken. For example, security should not be tightened unexpectedly, locks and access passwords should not be changed, and new policies pertinent to the crime under investigation should not be introduced.

Involvement of law enforcement agents
A law enforcement agent should be involved in an undercover investigation if the investigation results in legal prosecution. Besides, a law enforcement agent can supervise undercover investigations concerned with drug

Copyright © Mometrix Media. You have been licensed one copy of this document for personal use only. Any other reproduction or redistribution is strictly prohibited. All rights reserved.

possession, abuse, and distribution, since private investigators are not authorized to possess, purchase, or transport illegal drugs. Another aspect of undercover investigations a law enforcement agent can assist with is ensuring the criminal immunity for private investigators. In this case, the officer should have prior knowledge of the private investigator's engagement in illegal activity. Although law enforcement officers can offer substantial help and protection to the private undercover investigator, it is usually implied that in exchange for this protection, the private investigator should contribute a part of his/her efforts to solving bigger community problems under police jurisdiction.

Attorney involvement

An attorney plays an important role in an undercover workplace investigation as he/she is the main provider of the legal employment-related advice. The chosen attorney should be an expert in labor law, workplace negotiations and arbitration, employee discipline, and have an understanding of criminal law. Most of the attorney's duties should be allocated to assist the client in determining the further cause of action, such as ignoring the incident, using alternative means of dispute resolution, or pursue litigation. Besides, the presence of an attorney during meetings can ensure that the communications are protected under the client-attorney privilege. In case an attorney engages the investigator in the undercover operation, the case becomes protected as the attorney's work product and is not subject to discovery.

Substance abuse investigation

The steps of a substance abuse investigation include the following:
- Planning and preparation –great effort should be put into planning and preparation, as the success of the investigation largely depends on how well the investigation was planned and how well the investigator is prepared to conduct all the necessary activities
- Problem identification – correct identification of the problem ensures the success of the entire investigation
- Information collection – this method depends on the location of the workplace and other factors; methods include physical and electronic surveillance, research and audit, forensic analysis, interviewing, and undercover operations
- Verification and interpretation of information – through interviewing and analysis of witness statements and other evidence
- Recommendation for disciplinary and corrective action – the actions depend on the graveness of the evidence found
- Prevention and education – the final report is used to devise preventive measures and educate other employees and management.

Shoplifting

Shoplifting, or retail theft, is theft of retail merchandise in a shop, store, or other retail establishment, by a perpetrator posing as a customer. Shoplifters are divided into several categories: a) amateurs, b) juvenile, c) professional, d) kleptomaniacs, and e) drug and alcohol addicts. The reasons for shoplifting include: impulse, peer pressure, desperation, revenge, or behavioral disorder. Shoplifters may present the following statements as rationalization for their actions:

Copyright © Mometrix Media. You have been licensed one copy of this document for personal use only. Any other reproduction or redistribution is strictly prohibited. All rights reserved.

- Shoplifting is borrowing, not stealing.
- Everybody does it.
- Shoplifting is morally correct.
- Shoplifting is a reward for the job.
- Shoplifting is a legal political act in a social class struggle.
- Most of the shoplifters are amateurs, although there are professional shoplifters who are more skilled and therefore more difficult to catch.

Signs of a shoplifter

The following are some of the signs of potential shoplifters:
- Individuals wearing heavy oversized coats out of season
- Individuals wearing baggy pants and full skirts out of current trend
- Individuals displaying darting eye movement
- Individuals carrying many supermarket bags, large backpacks and purses
- Individuals leaving the store in a hurry
- Customers who are not certain what they want and seem uninterested in merchandise they asked for
- Individuals who leave the store clutching a pile of bags close to the body
- Customers who seem uninterested and claim that they are waiting for someone
- Customers who make an effort to distract sales clerks to conceal their actions
- A group of customers trying many items together in one fitting room.

Prevention

The following methods can be used to prevent shoplifting:
- Training store employees to recognize signs of potential shoplifters

- Offering employees rewards for deterring shoplifters
- Requiring employees to greet each person walking into the store
- Maximizing visibility of all areas in the store by using closed circuit TV cameras, one-way and convex mirrors, raising the cash registry area, and optimizing the store layout
- Using surveillance cameras
- Posting anti-shoplifting warning signs
- Reinforce the cash registry monitoring
- Keeping the cash registry locked at all times
- Requiring cashiers to staple the receipt to the bag
- Monitoring delivery personnel
- Requiring cashiers to check every item sold that might hide stolen items.

Operative placement in undercover company investigations

For the operative placement to look natural, precautions should be followed. As few people within the company as possible should know about the real activity of the new employee. Only those that absolutely have to know should be informed, for example, the senior human resources manager. One of the following methods of hiring should be used:
- A cold hire, which means that the human resources management is unaware that the new employee is an undercover operative
- A controlled hire, which means that the human resources manager is instructed to hire the operative.

The cover position for the operative should not be task related and should allow him/her to move around the facilities freely and have the least amount of supervision. It is imperative that the

Copyright © Mometrix Media. You have been licensed one copy of this document for personal use only. Any other reproduction or redistribution is strictly prohibited. All rights reserved.

operative should be placed in the area where the goods are being stolen to ensure the maximum exposure to the suspected perpetrator.

Auto theft claim assessment

Before taking on an auto theft investigation, the investigator should asses the claim for potential fraud. The following factors should be examined in order to determine the validity of the claim:

- The claimant's address stated as a hotel, motel, or bar
- Accessibility of the claimant
- The claimant's family members unawareness of the theft or loss
- The claimant's reluctance to use US Postal Service
- The claimant's income incompatibility with the cost of the lost vehicle
- The claimant's age and sex
- The claimant's employment status
- The claimant's unfulfilled financial obligation to the lienholder
- The claimant's insurance history
- The claimant's signs of impatience in resolving the claim.

Fuel theft investigation

The main method of detecting fuel theft involves adding a foreign substance to the fuel. The recommended ingredients for the substance are a 5 percent solution of sodium carbonate and phenolphthalein. To identify and trace the fuel, follow these steps:

- Place 3 pints of untreated fuel into the half-gallon bottle. Add ½ ounce of sodium carbonate solution. Close and shake the bottle for 2 minutes. Examine the water layer at the bottom. Empty and wash the bottle.
- Place 1 ounce of phenolphthalein for each 10,000 gallons of fuel in a

quart bottle. Fill ¾ of the bottle with alcohol. Seal and shake the bottle until the chemical is dissolved.
- Place 2 pints of tagged fuel into the half-gallon bottle. Add ½ ounce of sodium carbonate solution. Close and shake the bottle for 2 minutes. Examine the water layer at the bottom; it should be pink.

Workplace violence

The causes of workplace violence include employment-related stress, such as imminent unemployment, internal conflicts, work overload; substance abuse; and external conflicts, such as divorce and abusive relationships. Before starting a workplace violence investigation, the investigator should determine if the situation is dangerous enough for immediate law enforcement assistance. If there has been a physical attack, it is necessary to obtain an arrest warrant. If there are no signs of immediate danger, the first step is to conduct workplace interviews to determine the type of relationships between the perpetrator and the victim. The status of both individuals should be identified; the co-workers and management should be interviewed to find out if there are witnesses of the incident. The witnesses' statements should be collected and documented. The investigator's findings should be presented in a report, which is used as a basis for further disciplinary action or legislation.

Sexual harassment investigations

Sexual harassment is defined as an explicitly sexual, repetitive act that is unsolicited and unwelcome by the victim. Before starting a sexual harassment investigation, the investigator must make

Copyright © Mometrix Media. You have been licensed one copy of this document for personal use only. Any other reproduction or redistribution is strictly prohibited. All rights reserved.

sure that the employer was aware of the occurrence of this act and did not take any counteraction. Methods of investigating sexual harassment include surveillance of the alleged perpetrator, interviews of co-workers and management, interviews of the victim, and an interrogation of the alleged perpetrator. The investigator should attempt to persuade the perpetrator to admit his/her misconduct during the interrogation. As soon as all the necessary information has been obtained, the investigator should present his/her findings in a report. The report will aid the management in determining the occurrence of the sexual harassment act, collecting further information for the pertinent employment decision, deciding on a disciplinary act or litigation, reducing damages brought by the complaint, and preventing future acts.

Due diligence investigations

Due diligence investigation is a term that refers to an investigation that is used to verify and uncover information on acquisitions and mergers, client representations, personal and corporate debt collections, insurance underwriting, intellectual property, business or real property sales, etc. The purpose of due diligence investigations is to determine if the plaintiff can collect in case litigation is pursued and to estimate the potential collection. The main method employed in due diligence investigations is a review of financial history which can be facilitated through investigative research, workplace interviews, and searches. In corporate due diligence investigations business transactions, corporate purchases, and other business activity is examined. The main objective is to assess a person's or a corporation's means against their ability. Sometimes it is necessary to use international affiliates as the investigation may extend beyond the territory of the US.

Arson

Motives for arson are as follows:
- Financial gain by the owner of the destroyed property, for example insurance.
- An attempt to destroy property in order to eliminate or inhibit a competitor.
- Extortion by organized criminal organizations in order to intimidate and/or gain financial benefits.
- Revenge at management by employers in case of labor problems.
- Acts of vandalism, hate crime.
- An attempt to destroy evidence pointing towards another crime.
- Acts of pyromaniacs.
- An attempt from a firefighter to gain a hero status by starting and responding to the fire. A plausible reason when there is evidence that the alleged suspect made remarks about his heroic behavior.

The following evidence can point towards arson:
- Evidence of planning, such as removing furniture and equipment from the building, increase of insurance coverage.
- Presence of evidence of another crime.
- Evidence of participation.
- Evidence of exclusive access.

The most important steps in arson cases are:
- Identification of an individual who first noticed the fire.
- Identification of an individual who first called in the fire.
- Identification of color of flames and smoke.
- Search for signs of explosion before the fire.

Copyright © Mometrix Media. You have been licensed one copy of this document for personal use only. Any other reproduction or redistribution is strictly prohibited. All rights reserved.

- Search for any suspicious circumstances or unusual conditions.
- Identification of victims.
- Identification of individuals who had access to the site.
- Identification of the owner of the property.
- Determination of the amount of the insurance, the name and contact information of the insurance company.
- Inventory of items destroyed in the fire.
- Identification of the individual who took photos or video of the fire scene.
- Identification of Fire Department personnel who responded to the fire.
- Identification of equipment used to extinguish the fire.
- Evidence collection and preservation.
- Identification and interview of witnesses.
- Debriefing of all parties involved in the fire.

Burglary

Burglary is a term that refers to the illegal breaking and entering of private property with the intent to commit a felony, usually theft. There are several types of burglary:
- Unarmed burglary
- Armed burglary with assault
- Burglary of the building, vehicle, or vessel with the intent to commit misdemeanor
- Burglary of the building, vehicle, or vessel with the intent to commit destruction of valuables
- Burglary with the intent to commit a felony causing fear in the person residing in the dwelling
- Burglary with the intent to commit a felony without causing fear in the person residing in the dwelling
- Possession, production, and handling of burglarious instruments.

The most important steps in burglary cases are:
- Identification of location of the burglarized site.
- Description of the burglarized site.
- Documentation of time, date, and circumstances of burglary.
- Compilation of an itemized list of stolen property.
- Identification and description of exact location of all the items taken.
- Description of physical evidence found at the scene.
- Identification of the individual who reported the burglary.
- Documentation of the date and time the burglary was reported.
- Identification and interviewing of witnesses.
- Collection of information on individuals who had access to or visited the site.
- Collection of information on potential frauds.
- Identification of serial numbers, tags, and other marks of all items of stolen property.
- Description of the modus operandi of the burglary, that is, method of entry and exit, methods of search, time of the day, etc.

Robbery

Robbery is a term that refers to a serious criminal offence that involves forcefully taking money or property of another individual by instilling fear or using violence. Robberies often result in murder. There are several types of robbery:

Copyright © Mometrix Media. You have been licensed one copy of this document for personal use only. Any other reproduction or redistribution is strictly prohibited. All rights reserved.

- Armed robbery – use of a weapon for intimidating or assaulting the victim
- Masked robbery – use of a mask to conceal the identity of a robber
- Unarmed robbery – robbery without the use of weapons
- Robbery with confining and instilling fear – intimidation of victim by restricting his/her freedom with subsequent larceny
- Attempted extortion – intimidation of the victim into surrendering the property willingly in order to avoid assault
- Unarmed assault with the intent of robbery
- Highway robbery – robbery in public or open places
- Carjacking – stealing vehicles while threatening the driver.

The following are the most important steps in robbery investigations:
- Checking the facilities' alarms for operating conditions.
- Determining if there was an unauthorized access to the property.
- Determining if the response to the robbery was associated with the alarm.
- Determining if the response authorities were in possession of the sketches of high value facilities.
- Checking the closed circuit TV for operating condition during the robbery.
- Identification and interview of the robbed facility staff.
- Evidence collection, marking, and preservation.
- Obtaining victim and witness statements.
- Compilation of the description of the suspect(s).
- Description of the modus operandi, that is, method of entry and exit, methods of search, time of the day, etc.
- Compilation of the itemized list of the property taken.
- Determining if there were any threats and assault made during the robbery.
- Photographing the scene.
- Notification of the property owner and a law enforcement agency.

Pedophile investigations

The following are the most important steps in pedophile investigations:
- Identification of laws and elements of laws that have been violated.
- Identification of the suspect.
- Verification of alibis.
- Identification of witnesses and description of their knowledge of the crime.
- Obtaining statements made by victims, although this can be difficult to achieve due to the nature of the crime.
- Evidence collection, marking, and preservation.
- Identification of the individuals who photographed or took videos of the events pertinent to the crime committed.
- Compiling the summaries of witnesses' contributions to the investigation.
- Application for search and arrest warrants.
- Notification of appropriate welfare organizations.
- Making recommendations for prevention or elimination of future offences.
- Holding a press conference to address media concerns.
- Protection of victims and witnesses.

- 39 -

Copyright © Mometrix Media. You have been licensed one copy of this document for personal use only. Any other reproduction or redistribution is strictly prohibited. All rights reserved.

Hate crime

Hate crime is a term that refers to any criminal offences targeted at individuals of a specific race, nationality, religion, sexual orientation, ethnicity, social origin, or handicap. The main motives for hate crime are biases and prejudices against various social groups. A distinguishing characteristic of a hate crime is that although it may be targeting one victim, the whole group to which this victim belongs is victimized. Also, hate crimes do not usually stop at a single incident, but cause a wave of subsequent crimes. Most hate crimes are committed by individuals who support stereotypes and act on impulse. Many hate crimes are committed by individuals who seek excitement by targeting random representatives of minorities. A smaller percentage of hate crimes is committed by the convinced bias-motivated offenders.

Gray goods investigation and prevention

The following laws can be applied to gray goods investigation and prevention:
- 18 US Code 1964 – Section 336, Section 338a, Section 338b, Section 396e, Section 408, Section 409, Section 419d.
- 28 US Code 1331 – "The district courts shall have original jurisdiction of all civil actions arising under the Constitution, laws, or treaties of the United States."
- 28 US Code 1332 – Diversity of citizenship, amount in controversy, costs.
- 18 US Code 1341 – Fines and imprisonment for mail fraud.
- 18 US Code 1343 – Fraud by wire, radio, or television.
- 18 US Code 2314 – Transportation of stolen goods, securities, moneys, fraudulent State tax stamps, or articles used in counterfeiting.
- 15 US Code 1114 – Remedies, infringement, innocent infringement by printers and publishers.
- 15 US Code 1125 – False designations of origin, false descriptions, dilution.

Constructive and reconstructive investigations

The differences between constructive and reconstructive investigations are their purposes and the time when they take place in relation to the crime. Constructive investigations take place when the criminal activity is currently occurring or when a crime is anticipated. All undercover investigations and surveillance operations fall under the category of constructive investigations. If a person files a complaint about another person's offensive demeanor, the investigation that follows the complaint is also constructive. The purpose of constructive investigations is to determine if the criminal activity is actually taking place. Reconstructive investigations occur after the incident or the crime has already occurred. The purpose of reconstructive investigations is to recreate the incident in order to understand what happened. All overt investigations fall under the category of reconstructive.

Copyright © Mometrix Media. You have been licensed one copy of this document for personal use only. Any other reproduction or redistribution is strictly prohibited. All rights reserved.

Evidence Collection

Surveillance

Surveillance is a process of monitoring the subject's behavior where the subject may be a person, a group of people, an object, a location, or a process. Surveillance can be mobile or stationary; conducted with or without the help of technology, such as automobiles, aircraft, and various visual, audio, and video devices. Surveillance can be continuous, that is, continue for a long period of time, usually 24 hours a day; or it can be periodic, that is, conducted during specific periods of time. Surveillance can have different levels of intensity. The purpose of surveillance in the investigation is to obtain corroborative information to confirm suspicions and potentially identify the suspect. Surveillance can also be used as a preventive method. The following types of investigations may require surveillance: relationship (cheating), child custody, worker's compensation and insurance claims, employee theft, bounty hunting.

The following are the most common methods of surveillance:
- Foot – following the subject on foot.
- Single-vehicle – following the moving subject or vehicle in a single vehicle.
- Multiple-vehicle – following the moving subject or vehicle in multiple vehicles in order to stay undetected by the subject.
- Aerial – following and monitoring the moving vehicle or subject from an aircraft, such as an airplane or a helicopter.
- Vehicle tracking – detection of the moving or stationary vehicle with a tracking device attached to the vehicle.
- Tracking into private places – detection of the moving subject with a tracking device attached to a movable object carried by the subject.
- Thermal Imaging – detection of heat sources with forward-looking infrared devices (FLIRs).
- Direct observation – monitoring the subject without surveillance devices.
- Visual – monitoring of subjects with binoculars, telescopes, or night-vision devices.
- Audio – intercepting conversations with concealed microphones and wiretaps.
- Video – recording subjects with covert or overt video devices.

<u>Types of surveillance</u>
There are two types of surveillance: mobile and stationary. Mobile surveillance is used to detect moving subjects or objects, for example vehicles, or movable items carried by the subject. Mobile surveillance is most effective when used to track suspects and suspicious vehicles, to lead to the potential crime scenes or places of criminal activity. Mobile surveillance can be conducted on foot or with the help of tailing vehicles, aircraft, thermal imaging and tracking devices. Stationary surveillance is used to monitor fixed subjects or places. Stationary surveillance is most effective when used to observe employees' behavior at work, people's behavior at home, public places, etc. Also, buildings, offices, other public and private locations can be monitored to detect signs of suspicious or criminal activity. Stationary surveillance can be conducted by direct observation or with the help of various visual, audio, and video devices.

Surveillance and undercover investigation

The difference between surveillance and undercover investigation lies in purpose, objectives, and functions of the investigator. The purpose of surveillance is to follow the subject or watch an area and collect observations on behavior and activities. The purpose of an undercover investigation is not only to observe but also to make subjects react to certain behaviors or activities, or interact with an investigator or other subjects in a specific way. The objective of surveillance is to collect evidence, while the objective of an undercover investigation is to expose and possibly detain the suspect. The functions of the investigator in surveillance require him or her to stay concealed while performing the operation. The functions of the investigator in an undercover investigation require his or her exposure while playing a role.

Counter surveillance operations and equipment

The following are some of the most common counter surveillance operations and equipment:

- Sweep – an inspection of a place, such as a room or a building, for the presence of bugging devices.
- Bug detector – an electronic device that produces an audio tone that picks up any electronic transmission and pinpoints the exact location of bugs.
- Phone tap detection device – an electronic device that indicates the presence of wiretap in the phone.
- Camera detection device – works similar to bug detector indicating the presence of concealed video cameras.
- Scrambler – an electronic device attached to a telephone that makes the speaker's voice appear distorted to every listener except the one who has a similar device coded to receive the normal voice.
- White noise blocker – a device that acts like an electromagnetic megaphone attempting to drown out the user's desired signal.

Overt and covert surveillance

Covert surveillance implies that the investigator does not reveal his/her identity or the surveillance operation to the subject. All surveillance operations are covert in nature, and many of them require the investigators to practice their skills in concealing their activities. Overt surveillance implies that the subject is informed and has given consent to participate in the operation. Still, the subject may not necessarily know the identity of the investigator. The overt surveillance may be used for the following purposes:

- To prevent criminal activity or incidents
- To reduce number of crimes and incidents
- To cause the subject to react in a certain way or engage in certain behavior in order to obtain more information.

Reasons for surveillance

Surveillance is conducted for the following reasons:

- To collect information to justify a search warrant
- To monitor locations for signs of criminal activity
- To detect the presence of an ongoing criminal activity
- To identify and capture a suspect
- To gather intelligence
- To collect more information on witnesses and other individuals the subject is associated with

Copyright © Mometrix Media. You have been licensed one copy of this document for personal use only. Any other reproduction or redistribution is strictly prohibited. All rights reserved.

- To find stolen property, for example vehicles
- To collect information to be later used in an interview or interrogation
- To monitor equipment, such as computer screens, for fraudulent activity
- To prevent crimes and incidents in public places, such as intersections, entrances and exits of the banks and retail stores.

Audio surveillance equipment

The following belong to the group of audio surveillance equipment:
- Sound Monitors – devices that pick up sound, such as conversations, in rooms. Sound monitors can be activated and controlled over a touch-tone phone.
- Sound Recorders – audio devices used to record conversations and other sounds on an electronic or digital storage device, such as an audio tape or a digital disk.
- Telephone Conversation Recorders – devices attached or embedded in a telephone, used to listen to and record telephone conversations.
- Wire Tapping Devices – devices that intercept a telephone conversation by accessing the telephone signal itself.
- Electronic Eavesdropping Devices – listening and recording devices that use electronic transmission to monitor conversations.
- Parabolic Microphone – a listening device that transmits long-distance conversations (up to 300 feet) by using acoustical amplification.
- Audio Surveillance through the Internet devices – listening and recording devices that transmit sound over the Internet connection.

Mobile surveillance equipment

The following belong to the group of mobile surveillance equipment:
- Tailing vehicles – cars and other transportation used to follow the subject or the suspicious vehicle. Tailing vehicles may or may not be equipped with tracking devices.
- Small-sized aircraft – airplanes and helicopters which may or may not be equipped with vehicle tracking devices.
- Vehicle tracking devices – various types of GPS systems used to monitor the subject's movement. A tracking device consists of three components: a source generating a signal, a sensor receiving the signal, and a control box processing and interpreting the signal.
- Object tracking devices – micro and stick GPS systems that can be attached to small items carried by the subject under surveillance.
- Thermal imaging devices – forward-looking infrared devices (FLIRs) which sense infrared energy that varies with the temperature of objects in a scene and then generate a thermal signature image.

Visual surveillance equipment

The following belong to the group of visual surveillance equipment:
- Binoculars – viewing devices capable of medium magnification, usually used for short distances.
- Telescopes – viewing devices capable of large magnification, used for long distances.

Copyright © Mometrix Media. You have been licensed one copy of this document for personal use only. Any other reproduction or redistribution is strictly prohibited. All rights reserved.

- Image enhancing night-vision binoculars – viewing devices capable of detecting objects in the dark by amplifying bits of light, including the lower segment of the infrared light spectrum.
- Thermal imaging night-vision binoculars – viewing devices capable of detecting objects in the dark by reacting to the heat emitted by objects and capturing the upper segment of the infrared light spectrum.
- Aqua binoculars – viewing devices capable of detecting objects in water by using the protective coat on the lenses.

Video surveillance equipment

The following belong to the group of video surveillance equipment:
- Video Recorders – devices that record video and store the footage on analog or digital devices, such as video tape or digital disk.
- Analog – devices that record and transmit video through closed circuit television.
- IP-based Video Cameras – devices that transmit video through Local Area Network (LAN) to a server or a computer.
- DVR (Digital Video Recorder) – a device that records and stores digital video.
- Monitors – analog or digital screens that display video transmitted from a camera.
- Wireless Camera Systems – systems complete with digital cameras and monitors that transmit video through wireless connection.
- Computer Monitoring Systems – systems complete with cameras, wireless transmitters, and recording software that take and store screen captures of a

computer monitor as well as URLs of web pages, keystrokes, etc.

Photo surveillance

The requirements for photo surveillance equipment are as follows:
- Camera should be 35mm single lens flex or digital to ensure the proper quality of images.
- Lenses should be 50 mm, plus additional wide angle, telephoto, close-up, and macro lenses. The objectives of surveillance determine the need for special lenses.
- Electronic flash should accompany the camera in case of taking photos in unfavorable light conditions. Batteries should be provided for the flash.
- Film or storage disk. The type of film depends on the conditions of light during photography. All digital cameras are equipped with a memory stick and a reading device that allows the transfer of images to a computer.
- Tripod to use for stationary shots. Make sure that tripod is sturdy and easy to use.
- Computer, image editing software, and printer to download, process, and print digital camera images.

Digital cameras
The following are the main advantages of using digital cameras in visual surveillance:
- Easy electronic storage on a portable disk or a computer hard drive
- Photos are immediately available for viewing
- Convenience of use
- Easy and quick printing
- Capability to digitally enlarge or enhance images in any other way (brighten, sharpen, focus)

Copyright © Mometrix Media. You have been licensed one copy of this document for personal use only. Any other reproduction or redistribution is strictly prohibited. All rights reserved.

- Easy and quick sharing by publishing on a website or sending in an email.

The following are some of the disadvantages of using digital cameras:
- Necessity to have the complete set of equipment, such as computer, software, and printer
- Necessity to have computer skills in order to process digital images
- High cost of computer equipment.

Pre-surveillance preparation

The following are the steps for pre-surveillance preparation:
- Information collection – gathering facts about the subject's habits, daily routines, work schedule, people he/she meets, transportation he/she uses, clothes he/she wears, places he/she visits, etc.
- Emotional preparation – patience, leadership skills, presence of mind, ability to make decisions on the spot.
- Physical needs preparation – equipping oneself for long hours without the ability to leave for food, drink, or toilet.
- Cover story preparation – preparing a disguise story if someone gets suspicious.
- Equipment set up – inspection and installation of all the equipment to be used in surveillance.
- Temporary headquarters or telephone base establishment – setting up a temporary base for debriefing in case of surveillance termination or any other reason.
- Police notification – informing the local police about the planned surveillance.

- Blending – disguising oneself to look inconspicuous in the area of surveillance.
- Convoy awareness – preparing for a possibility of the subject sending a convoy to evade surveillance.

Blending into surveillance area

To effectively blend into the area of surveillance, the investigator should familiarize him/herself with the common appearances of people living or visiting the area. The ideal surveillant should be medium built, of average size, and have no peculiar features or mannerisms. The dress should be appropriate to the location of surveillance. For example, surveillance of a company headquarters requires a suit and a briefcase; casual clothes are more appropriate for retail premises, or industrial locations. It is recommended to carry newspapers, paperbacks, or magazines to appear distracted and not watching the subject. It is not recommended to bring amateur friends or family members as they might compromise the secrecy of the operation.

Vehicles in stationary surveillance

Since stationary surveillance might continue for indefinitely long periods of time, use of vehicles often comes as an advantage due to the following reasons:
- Vehicles are easier to blend into the area.
- Vehicles are more cost effective than rent of a house or an apartment.
- Vehicles can be stationed close to the subject's location.
- Large vehicles, such as vans and trucks provide space for concealed surveillance equipment such as receivers, computers, etc.
- Large vehicles also provide space for storage of food, drink, and portable toilet.

Copyright © Mometrix Media. You have been licensed one copy of this document for personal use only. Any other reproduction or redistribution is strictly prohibited. All rights reserved.

- Vehicles with tinted windows provide the opportunity for photographing and videotaping without the risk of being discovered.
- Specialty surveillance vans are equipped with periscopes which allow photographs to be taken in a 360-degree circumference.

Equipment setup for surveillance

The surveillant should focus on the following main points when setting up the equipment to be used in surveillance:
- The vehicle or vehicles should be checked for fuel, battery, and mechanical problems.
- If there are multiple vehicles to be used in surveillance, all their radio transmitters should be checked for functionality.
- Any type of transmitting devices should be checked for batteries, secure wiring, and functionality.
- New equipment should be tested for full functionality and battery charge.
- Video cameras and still cameras should be checked for lens integrity and cleanliness.
- Attachable devices should be tested for adhesiveness.
- Recording devices should be tested for sound emission.
- Devices that transmit over the Internet should be tested for stable connection.
- Surveillance software should be tested for functionality and compatibility.

Surveillant actions in case of discovery

In case the subject discovered the "tail" or the surveillant has suspicions that he/she has been noticed, this particular surveillant should discontinue participating in the operation. If possible he/she should notify the other surveillants, in case it is multiple-person or vehicle surveillance. The discovered surveillant should make sure he/she is not being followed by the subject to his/her home or office. To do this, the surveillant should make evasive moves and maneuver to the places where it is easier to get lost. Public places such as crowded streets, supermarkets, and train stations are preferred areas for disappearing. If surveillant had partners, surveillance should continue unless there is a suspicion that all the participants have been discovered.

ABC method of foot surveillance

The shadow method of foot surveillance presents a higher risk as it is easier to notice a one-person tail. The three-person foot surveillance, or the ABC method, significantly lowers the risk of being discovered. Person A is the closest to the subject. Person B follows Person A, on the same side of the street. Person C might be positioned on either the other side of the street or in front of the subject. At predetermined intervals all three persons, A, B, and C, change positions to reduce the risk of being noticed. Person A might relocate to the other side of the street, Person B might shift to the front of the subject, and Person C might take up the A's initial position.

Attention in surveillance operations

Attention is a psychological process of concentrating one's mental power on an object. Attention plays a very important role in surveillance because it is an essential constituent of the observation skills. Attention can be involuntary, voluntary, and habitual. Involuntary attention is awareness of the presence of an object without any mental effort. Involuntary attention is a product of the natural reactions of the five senses. The voluntary attention requires a mental

Copyright © Mometrix Media. You have been licensed one copy of this document for personal use only. Any other reproduction or redistribution is strictly prohibited. All rights reserved.

effort and a control over the five senses. The habitual attention is a product of training and requires little mental effort as the senses have been previously accustomed to become aware of certain signals. The voluntary attention is the one the surveillant uses to make observations. Since it demands control over one's senses, it is important for the investigator to train his/her sight, hearing, touch, taste, and smell for the signs of anything unusual or suspicious.

Covert surveillance in undercover theft investigations

Covert surveillance can be used to obtain corroborating evidence on videotape. The undercover investigator can act as a buyer and purchase some of the property that the thief is trying to resell. The surveillance team should be notified ahead of time to be ready with the surveillance van. The parking lot at the company premises serves as a good spot to stage and videotape the purchase because it provides a safe enough environment and allows for the covert operation to be staged without interference. The purchase should be carefully planned in order to include the documentation of the thief's identity, stolen property, the act of selling, etc. The employers or the law enforcement officers can participate in the surveillance operation as eyewitnesses to strengthen credibility of the evidence. If the state laws permit the voice recording, the conversations should be recorded to present a stronger case.

Covert undercover workplace investigation

The use of covert undercover investigation in the workplace is justified in the following cases:
- When there is a reliable information suggesting that one or several employees might be involved in criminal or civil misconduct, but there is not enough information to establish the identity of deviant employees or to stop the criminal activity.
- When there appear to be significant losses in a specific area but there is no information to rationalize or explain the losses.
- There is a suspicion on the part of more than one employee or supervisor of workplace alcohol or drug abuse, but there is not enough evidence.
- There is a necessity to monitor the employee's compliance with the company's policies and procedures, but it is impossible to conduct an audit.

Post-surveillance debriefing

Debriefing is a meeting held by the surveillance team after the surveillance is completed. The following aspects should be discussed during the debriefing:
- Things that went right.
- Things that went wrong.
- Alternative methods for future surveillance operations.
- Possible solutions for future problems.
- Learning outcomes.
- The team leader should collect reports from all the other members of the surveillance team and share the results with everyone. After that, the whole team discusses the issues that arose during the operation, proposing alternative moves and solutions.

The purpose of post-surveillance debriefing is to learn from the experience of others on the surveillance team and generate new ideas for future surveillance operations.

Copyright © Mometrix Media. You have been licensed one copy of this document for personal use only. Any other reproduction or redistribution is strictly prohibited. All rights reserved.

Surveillance mistakes

The most serious mistakes made while conducting surveillance are:
- Assuming that the subject is going to spend a night at a hotel or a motel if he or she checked in during the p.m. hours or close to midnight.
- Assuming that the subject is going to exit the building the same way he or she entered it.
- Assuming that the subject is going to spend a night at home if he or she returned to his/her home or apartment.
- Assuming that the subject has discovered the surveillant if he or she starts to run or speeds up his/her vehicle.
- Using a conspicuous vehicle, such as expensive vehicles in poor neighborhoods, or vice versa.
- Making repeating phone calls from the same location.
- Keeping the vehicle parked in the same location for conspicuously long periods of time.

Person descriptions

The following are the details that should be mentioned in an accurate person description:
- Voice – pitch, accent, intensity.
- Body scars and marks – location, size, shape.
- Dress – color, cost, condition.
- Sex – male or female, disguised or not.
- Race – Caucasian, African-American, Native American, Hispanic, Asian, etc.
- Age – in increments of five.
- Height – within two inches.
- Build – emaciated, thin, medium, stocky, obese.
- Face and head – shape, complexion.
- Hair – color, hairline location, dyed or not, type of haircut, length.
- Eyebrows – shape, length, breadth, color.
- Eyes – size, color, shape, set, contacts, glasses.
- Nose – width, shape, line of the bridge.
- Mouth – size, shape, size and color of teeth, fullness of lips.
- Chin – size, shape, profile.
- Ears – size, shape.
- Neck – length and thickness.
- Shoulders – square or oblique, narrow or broad.
- Hands – size, shape, fingers, rings.

Observation skills

In order to make accurate observations, the investigator should continually train him/herself in the following activities:
- Developing full awareness and alertness to everything that is going on around him/her
- Paying full attention to even the minutest details
- Developing the habit of observing details and not generalities
- Developing an accurate sense of time, distance, speed, direction, age
- Developing the ability to distinguish between colors, hues, tones, and shades, as well as intensity and saturation of color
- Developing the ability to visualize events, objects, and persons
- Developing the ability to listen carefully and interpret sounds in various settings
- Developing the ability to identify smells
- Developing the ability to distinguish between various textures.

Copyright © Mometrix Media. You have been licensed one copy of this document for personal use only. Any other reproduction or redistribution is strictly prohibited. All rights reserved.

Subject identification form

The subject identification form which is distributed before the surveillance operation should contain the following information:

- Full name and alias.
- Date of birth.
- Phone numbers, such as home, work, cell.
- Home and work address.
- Work schedule, that is, daily hours, break hours, etc.
- All possible routes to and from work, and to and from home.
- Vehicle description including type, color, and license plate number.
- Description of the subject including height, weight, build, color of eyes, hair, race, age.
- Habits, such as smoking, drinking, drugs.
- Driving habits, including speeding.
- Associates, such as friends, co-workers, customers, service providers.
- Places the subject visits frequently, for example, bars, stores, restaurants, hotels, public offices.
- Objectives of surveillance.
- Warning of any dangerous environments or activities.
- Requirements for restricted communication.

Vehicle descriptions

The following are the details that should be mentioned in an accurate vehicle description:

- Type – sedan, two-door, four-door, pickup truck, convertible, SUV, van, mini-van, trailer, commercial vehicle, motorcycle, scooter, bicycle.
- Size – large, medium, small.
- Color – precise hue, dark or light, custom paint jobs, decorations.

- Year – in increments of ten, although might be difficult to determine.
- Make and model – domestic or foreign, for example, Ford Escort, Pontiac Trans Am, Toyota Corolla, Mercedes-Benz 300E.
- License Plate number.
- Condition – old, new, excellent, good, fair, poor, junk.
- Peculiar characteristics – dents, scratches, shattered wind shields, corrosion, missing parts, tires, custom accessories, for example spoilers, radiators, etc., interior, such as leather or fabric, clean or littered.

Report

Report is a term that is used to describe the investigator's awareness and understanding of the fact during observation. Report also relates to naming facts as they are observed. Three factors affect the investigator's report:

- Vocabulary
- Time lag
- Intervening recurrences of similar events.

Vocabulary affects the accuracy of the verbal account of the facts observed. The investigator should possess adequate vocabulary to be able to report and describe the events exactly as they occurred. Time lag might prevent the investigator from reporting the facts accurately. The longer is the period of time between the observation and the report, the more difficult it is to give an accurate account of events. Intervening recurrences of similar events might prevent the investigator from noticing and reporting the facts. Unusually unique events are easier to notice, memorize, and identify, whereas routine acts are not.

- 49 -

Copyright © Mometrix Media. You have been licensed one copy of this document for personal use only. Any other reproduction or redistribution is strictly prohibited. All rights reserved.

Surveillance law landmarks

The following are landmarks in surveillance case law history:

- 1928, Olmstead vs. US – the prosecuted bootleggers accused federal agents of intercepting their telephone conversations thus violating their Fourth Amendment rights.
- 1952, On Lee vs. US, and 1963, Lopez vs. United States – federal undercover agents were accused of wearing illegal concealed transmitters. The U.S. Supreme Court ruled that the use of transmitters did not violate the Constitution.
- 1967, Berger vs. New York – the Court ruled that the use of bugs and wiretaps did not violate laws in states which had legislation authorizing the use of concealed listening and recording devices and where officers obtained a warrant.
- 1967, Katz vs. US – the Court ruled that the warrant must be obtained for intercepting a private conversation occurring in a public place if the person engaged in the conversation makes an indication to keep it private.
- 2001, Kyllo vs. US – the Court ruled that the use of electronic surveillance may require a warrant if applied toward private residencies.

The following are landmarks of surveillance legislative law history:

- 1968 – Congress passed Title III of the Omnibus Crime Control and Safe Streets Act, 18 U.S.C. 2510-2520. The Act prohibits police officers to intercept wire and oral communication in all circumstances except: a) one of the parties' consent was obtained,
  b) the court order was issued, or
  c) the interception is used in cases of organized crime and national security.
- 1986 – Congress enacted the Electronics Communications Privacy Act. The Act regulates the recent, more sophisticated, forms of electronic surveillance, such as covert video cameras, tracking devices, etc. The Act requires police officers to obtain court orders before using such devices. Officers failing to abide by this law are subjected to criminal and civil penalties.
- 1994 – Congress enacted the Communications Assistance for Law Enforcement Act. The Act requires telephone companies to assist police officers in their electronic surveillance of organized crime and terrorists by modifying their digital technology.

Ex parte order

Ex parte order is the court order that permits the electronic interception of oral or wire communication through bugs, body mikes, wiretaps, and other devices. The order remains in effect only for the period necessary to achieve the objective of surveillance and does never allow any operations longer than thirty days. However, the order can be granted an indefinite number of extensions. Ex parte orders always contain a minimization requirement. The requirement commands surveillants to monitor only those conversations that are directly related to the criminal or fraudulent activity under investigation. The interception should be immediately terminated as soon as the conversation ceases to relate to the crime or fraud.

Copyright © Mometrix Media. You have been licensed one copy of this document for personal use only. Any other reproduction or redistribution is strictly prohibited. All rights reserved.

Legislative principles of ethical surveillance

In order not to breach the Fourth Amendment, it is recommended that surveillance is conducted according to the following principles:

- Surveillance should not be conducted or used in such a way that it infringes on a person's legitimate expectation of privacy.
- Surveillance must be undertaken only for a justifiable purpose.
- Surveillance must be conducted in a manner appropriate for its purpose.
- Surveillance user should be identified in notice provisions.
- Surveillance user is considered accountable for his/her surveillance devices, obtained evidence, and the consequences of their use.
- Surveillance users must ensure the safety of all aspects of their surveillance system.
- Evidence obtained through surveillance must be used in a fair manner and only for the purpose obtained.
- Evidence obtained through surveillance must be destroyed within a specified period upon the completion of the investigation.

Fourth Amendment violation

Electronic surveillance is considered a violation of the Fourth Amendment when it is used in a manner that infringes an individual's reasonable expectation of privacy. The use of any covert electronic devices that threaten the people's right to maintain safety of their houses, or keep their papers and possessions secure violates the Fourth Amendment. Anything that can be classified as an unreasonable search and seizure breaches the people's constitutional right to remain safe in their persons. Therefore, the investigator and the court should establish a reasonable cause to issue a warrant to conduct electronic surveillance. The investigator has to bring solid proof to justify the surveillance, describing the place to be observed, and the possible nature of conversations or activity to be intercepted. The court has to use its reason and common sense to evaluate this proof and issue the warrant.

Crime scene and crime scene processing

Crime scene is a term that can be applied to the following:

- The area where a crime has been committed
- The area surrounding the immediate perimeter of the place where the crime has been committed
- The area where the evidence of the crime has been found
- The crime scene can be extended from the area where the crime has been committed to the area where the suspect has been apprehended.

Crime scene processing is the initial step of an investigation. It includes:

- Protection of the crime scene from contamination
- Preliminary scan
- Search for evidence
- Photographing
- Sketching and preparation of scale models
- Collection, packaging, and marking of evidence
- Reconstruction of the crime.

Crime scene processing in arson cases
During the crime scene processing the investigator should attempt to determine the presence of accelerants (substances that activate and speed up the fire). Thorough examination of debris at the

- 51 -

Copyright © Mometrix Media. You have been licensed one copy of this document for personal use only. Any other reproduction or redistribution is strictly prohibited. All rights reserved.

crime scene may reveal the presence of gasoline, explosives, fuel oil, and other substances or devices that may have been used to start the fire. Preserving the evidence at the scene of fire proves to be difficult because firefighters and medical personnel may destroy the evidence while making the efforts to stop the fire and rescue the victims. It is important to discover the point of origin of fire and determine the direction of the fire by examining the burning patterns on the walls, floor, and furniture. The main goal of the fire scene processing is to identify the incendiary material, such as gas, electric appliances, wiring, papers, clothing, cigarettes, candles, matchsticks, etc.

Duties at the crime scene

Investigator
The duties of the investigator at the crime scene consist of the following:
- Respond to the crime scene as soon as the first responding patrol officer requests the presence
- Interview the first responding patrol officer about possible suspects, witnesses, and the exact conditions of the crime scene at the moment of arrival
- Remind the first responding patrol officer to document the actions taken at the scene
- Ensure that the crime scene is not occupied by unauthorized personnel
- Ascertain that the crime scene is not contaminated and the evidence integrity is preserved
- Take charge of processing the crime scene
- Begin the investigation.
- The case, lead, or primary investigators control all investigative activities occurring at the crime scene.

First responding patrol officer
The duties of the first responding patrol officer at the crime scene consist of the following:
- Arrest the suspect if he or she is still present at the crime scene and if there is a probable cause for the arrest
- Locate and question possible witnesses at the crime scene
- Secure the entrances and exits to the crime scene in order to protect it from contamination and preserve the integrity of evidence – this involves both protecting the scene from others as well as abstaining from introducing any changes to the crime scene and any evidence
- Notify the supervisors and request the presence of an investigator and a criminalist
- Document the actions taken at the scene.

Criminalist
The duties of the criminalist, also called forensic technician or crime scene technician, consist of the following:
- Respond to the crime scene as soon as the first responding patrol officer requests the presence
- Ascertain that the crime scene is not occupied by unauthorized personnel and is not contaminated
- Ascertain that the evidence integrity is preserved
- Establish a temporary headquarters
- Collect, package, and mark the evidence
- Photograph the crime scene
- Make sketches and scale models for reconstruction of the crime
- Maintain the chain of custody
- Transport the evidence to the crime lab for further analysis

Copyright © Mometrix Media. You have been licensed one copy of this document for personal use only. Any other reproduction or redistribution is strictly prohibited. All rights reserved.

- Respond to the primary investigator's requests for additional evidence collections.

Crime scene rules

The most important crime scene rules are as follows:
- Do not establish the temporary headquarters at the crime scene.
- Do not touch anything in order to not introduce any changes to the crime scene.
- Keep a log of the names of all individuals present at the scene, including police officers and media representatives.
- Do not permit unnecessary visitors.
- Protect outdoor evidence from elements, such as heat, moisture, etc.
- Do not use cloth to wrap evidence containing fingerprints.
- Determine points of entry and exit as soon as possible.
- Examine the crime scene for latent fingerprints.
- First locate and process the objects touched by the suspect.
- Maintain the chain of custody for all pieces of evidence.

Collecting evidence

The steps of collecting evidence are as follows:
- Plan the search direction and prepare collection equipment.
- Set up an evidence control log system and establish an evidence collection point.
- Coordinate evidence collection techniques and procedures, such as appropriate packaging and marking.
- Document the receipt of all properly marked and packaged evidence on the evidence control

log indicating the time, location, and the identity of the collector.
- Categorize all collected evidence.
- Maintain the chain of custody of collected evidence at the scene.
- Verify the records of collected evidence with the evidence control log before leaving the scene.
- Document the chain of custody and hand the evidence over to the evidence clerk for secure temporary storage.
- Prepare laboratory analysis requests and transfer evidence to the laboratory.

Crime scene protection

The following are the methods of crime scene protection:
- Establishing a police line by securing the outside perimeter of the crime scene with police barriers and tape.
- Displaying the signs "Crime Scene – Do Not Enter" around the perimeter of the crime scene.
- Assigning a uniformed officer to patrol the perimeter of the crime scene.
- Assigning an officer to provide special protection of the crime scene from representatives of the press and other officers not connected to the investigation.
- Setting up a log-in point at the entrance to the crime scene and assigning an officer to record all visitors.
- Requiring of all officers at the scene to complete a report describing their involvement in the current investigation and giving details about their exact actions at the scene.
- Requiring of all visitors at the scene to submit samples of blood,

Copyright © Mometrix Media. You have been licensed one copy of this document for personal use only. Any other reproduction or redistribution is strictly prohibited. All rights reserved.

fingerprints, etc. for elimination purposes.

Prevention of loss, contamination, and alteration of evidence

To prevent loss of evidence, each item should be secured in a container, such as a pillbox or a plastic vial that can be sealed. Envelopes are usually not suitable for safekeeping as they may leak at the corners. To prevent contamination of evidence, the investigator must wear surgical gloves while collecting evidence. It is also recommended to use eyedroppers, vials, and syringe needles to collect fluids. Items collected at one location should be separated from items collected at a different location. Each piece of evidence should be placed in a separate container even if they come from the same place. Evidence collected at the scene should be separated from the evidence obtained from the suspect. To prevent alteration, evidence should be packed and marked according to the appropriate standards. Chain of custody procedures must be followed at all times by all personnel involved in collection and examination of evidence.

Evidence

There are several types of evidence. The most essential types are real evidence, direct evidence, and circumstantial evidence. Real evidence refers to tangible objects, such as vehicles, weapons, substances, stolen property, clothes, etc. For example, a gun, drugs, a handkerchief, all can be classified as real evidence. Real evidence must be labeled and stored correctly in order to be admitted in court. Direct evidence refers to evidence that was obtained through the five senses, that is sight, hearing, smell, touch, and taste. For example, a witness's account of events is direct evidence. Direct evidence must be documented in order to be admitted in court. Circumstantial

evidence is evidence that is based on assumption. It is not verified and usually cannot stand up in court.

Chain of custody

Chain of custody can be defined as a process of handling the evidence and ensuring its integrity. Chain of custody can also be described as a paper trail documenting the seizure, custody, control, transfer, analysis, and deposition of evidence. In practice, it means that an investigator must document the process of collecting and storing of evidence. The following should be included in the documentation:

- Date
- Time
- Location
- Circumstances under which the evidence is collected
- Identity of the evidence handler
- Duration of evidence custody
- Conditions of evidence storage
- Conditions of evidence transfer to subsequent custodians of each evidence.
- Each piece of evidence in the link should be documented chronologically in order to prove its authenticity in court.

Procedures for laboratory analysis
The following is the chain of custody procedures if the evidence has to be analyzed in a laboratory:

- Before collecting evidence, the investigator should contact the laboratory and review the chain of custody procedures with the laboratory technicians.
- The investigator/collector gathers, packages, and marks evidence.
- Immediately after collecting an individual piece of evidence, the chain of custody record sheet must be filled out.

Copyright © Mometrix Media. You have been licensed one copy of this document for personal use only. Any other reproduction or redistribution is strictly prohibited. All rights reserved.

- The records must contain the following: a) investigation number; b) investigator/collector identity; c) subsequent handler's identity; d) evidence number; e) evidence description; f) evidence location; g) circumstances of collection; h) condition of evidence; i) collection date; j) collection time; k) laboratory numbers.
- Upon completion of collection, the evidence should be transported to the laboratory for analysis. The identity of the person transporting the evidence must be recorded on the chain of custody record sheet.
- Upon arrival at the lab, the deliverer should obtain a record of the receipt of evidence.
- When the laboratory returns the analyzed evidence the proper record must be made in the chain of custody sheet.

Search warrants

The search warrant must be obtained prior to conducting the search. In order to obtain a search warrant it is necessary for federal law enforcement officers to fulfill the requirements of the Fourth Amendment. This means that officers must prove that they have a probable cause for their suspicion that a specific location contains evidence, and they must describe the evidence they expect to discover in that location. The existence of the crime scene serves as a solid enough justification of a probable cause to grant a search warrant. Descriptions of evidence may be generic, but they must name the objects expected to be found, for example, weapons, documents, blood, etc.

The following are the instances when it is permissible to obtain a search warrant after the search at the crime scene:

- Consent – the person who called for the police gives his/her consent for a search without requiring a search warrant. The person who gives consent must have legitimate access to the property to be searched for the operation to be constitutional.
- Emergency – there are three types of emergencies that permit searches without a search warrant; they are immediate threat to life and safety, destruction or displacement of evidence, and escape. When the immediate danger has passed, the search warrant is required to continue the search.
- Public place – if the crime scene is located in a public place, such as a train station, the search warrant is not required.
- Public view – if the evidence is located in public view the search warrant is not required.

Strip search technique

The strip search technique requires splitting the crime scene into rows. The investigator should walk in each row from one end of the scene to the other, carefully examining every inch for traces of evidence. Then he/she should turn around and walk the next row in the opposite direction continuing the search. This technique is optimal for outdoor searches and large open areas, for example search in the park, factory floor, etc. The strip search may require the assistance of several members of the investigative team. The main advantage of the strip search is that it allows the investigator to cover a vast space in minimum time if many searchers are involved.

Copyright © Mometrix Media. You have been licensed one copy of this document for personal use only. Any other reproduction or redistribution is strictly prohibited. All rights reserved.

Spiral search technique

The spiral search technique treats the crime scene as a giant circle. The investigator starts outside of the circle and moves inward while decreasing the diameter of his/her circular moves. The investigator can walk clockwise or counterclockwise. Just like the strip search, the spiral search technique is optimal for outdoors and open spaces where there are not a lot of obstacles. A team of searchers can usually do a more efficient job of the spiral technique than an individual investigator. The main advantage of the spiral search technique is that it allows the investigative team to embrace the whole area of the crime scene, from the farthest point to the center, in a single search.

Grid search technique

The grid search technique is conducted similarly to the strip search. The difference is that the investigative team walks in both directions. The crime scene is divided into series of perpendicular and parallel rows. The investigator starts at the beginning of the row, walks to the other end, turns around, moves to the next parallel row and walks in the opposite direction. At the same time, another investigator moves in the same way in the perpendicular row. One investigative team can move from North to South, while another moves from East to West. This technique is used for searches in very large areas. The main advantage of the grid search technique is that it allows the investigative team to revisit the areas that have been already searched and eliminate the chance of overlooking evidence.

Section search technique

The section search technique requires dividing the area of the crime scene into sections and assigning an investigator to conduct the search in each specific section. Upon the completion of the initial search, the section is reassigned to another investigator who conducts the search again in order to produce the best results possible. The search continues until it is established that there is no more evidence left in the section. This technique is optimal for large outdoor or indoor spaces that have a lot of obstacles, for example, apartment buildings, office buildings, residential areas, etc. The main advantage of the section search technique is that it allows the investigative team to search through an obstructed area quickly and efficiently.

Requirements for crime scene photography

In order to be acceptable in court, crime scene photography must fulfill the following requirements:

- Photographs must be numerous because there is only one chance to take photos of the scene as it was found.
- Each roll must have a photo that identifies it and indicates the case report number and other related information.
- The overall scene photos must be taken in overlapping technique, in clockwise direction.
- The sequence of photographs must be from general to specific, ranging from long shots to close-ups.
- A photographic log must be maintained, containing time and date, brief descriptions of each photo, and other pertinent technical information.
- The photo prints must be clearly marked similar to other pieces of evidence.
- Small pieces of evidence in outdoor photos must be circled.

Copyright © Mometrix Media. You have been licensed one copy of this document for personal use only. Any other reproduction or redistribution is strictly prohibited. All rights reserved.

Photographic evidence of traffic accidents

While collecting photographic evidence at the traffic accident scene it is important to follow these guidelines:
- Take photos of the overall scene, from points of approach of all involved vehicles to the point of impact
- Photograph exact positions of all vehicles, injured persons, and objects involved in the accident
- Take close-ups of each point of impact on each vehicle and damage to real property, if any
- Photograph road defects, obstructions on the pavement
- Take close-ups of the damage to each vehicle involved, from exterior and interior
- Take medium shots of skid marks
- Photograph debris, such as glass, tire tracks, pieces of metal and plastic.

Crime scene sketches

Crime scene sketches are line drawings and diagrams that accurately and proportionally depict the overall area of the scene. Sketches serve as supplemental tools in crime scene processing and are made immediately upon the discovery of the crime scene. The purposes of sketches include:
- Documenting the precise location and relationship of specific pieces of evidence to other pieces of evidence and surrounding objects
- Serving as a visual reference for investigators and witnesses
- Documenting conditions, such as distances, topography, paths of vehicles, movements of victims and suspects
- Serving as a visual aid for prosecutors, judges, and jury

- Assisting with questioning suspects and witnesses
- Eliminating redundant and misdirecting details.

The sketches should be made on graph paper using a clipboard, a twelve-inch ruler, and a soft leaded pencil. Sketches should not be covered with multiple notes, only those necessary to understand the content. Items depicted on the sketch should be marked in the legend. The legend can indicate such data as item identification, location, description, measurements, distances, etc. A sketch should contain the case number, type of investigation, location, time and date of the incident, and the investigator's name. A sketch should indicate the location of the incident in relation to the location of the witness. A sketch that is not made to scale should be marked as such.

Packaging containers for evidence

Packaging containers that can be used for specific types of evidence are as follows:
- Small dry objects can be placed in plastic containers, such as plastic bags, pillboxes, capsules, or vials.
- Damp objects must be placed in paper envelopes to protect from bacteria and fungi.
- Papers can be placed in paper envelopes.
- Powdery substances must be placed in paper envelopes with sealed sides and corners.
- Fiber must be placed in vials or pillboxes.
- Garments can be wrapped in paper or placed in plastic or paper bags.
- Tools and auto parts must be placed it sealed heavy paper or plastic bags.
- Large objects containing adhering small objects must be wrapped in paper and secured with plastic tape.

Copyright © Mometrix Media. You have been licensed one copy of this document for personal use only. Any other reproduction or redistribution is strictly prohibited. All rights reserved.

Marking evidence

To be accepted in court, all pieces of evidence found at the crime scene should be clearly marked. Marking helps the investigator prove that the evidence is the same as discovered at the scene and has not been tampered with. Following are the rules for marking the evidence:

- A system of special symbols, marks, and initials must be used.
- Marks can be written, scratched, or carved on the piece of evidence.
- Marks must be as small as possible while legible.
- Marks must not damage the evidence or its value.
- Evidence that cannot be marked directly must be packed in special containers.
- Evidence containers must be marked even if the evidence inside is marked.
- Large pieces of evidence must be marked with special tags.
- All pieces of evidence and their serial numbers must be recorded in all documents pertaining to the investigation.

Collecting, marking, and packing ammunition evidence

The following are the guidelines for collecting, marking, and packing ammunition evidence:

- Bullets fired – collect with tweezers with taped ends; mark with initials at base of nose of bullet; sides must not be marked; pack in soft tissue paper and place in a marked pillbox.
- Bullet and cartridge case (not fired) – collect with tweezers with taped ends; mark with initials, date, and numbers corresponding to numbers of chambers at the base of nose of the bullet; pack in the same way as bullets.

- Cartridge cases (fired) – collect with tweezers with taped ends at open end; mark inside of casing, or outside as close to front as possible; pack in the same way as bullets.
- Shot shells – collect in the same way as bullets; mark with initials on side of brass head of shell; roll in paper and place in individual paper envelopes.

Collecting, marking, and packing firearms evidence

The following are the guidelines for collecting, marking, and packing firearms evidence:

- Handgun – must be collected using surgical gloves and handled by the knurled portion of the handgrips; must be marked with initials in an inconspicuous place on the frame, removable parts should not be marked, revolver guns should be marked for fired shell positions; must be labeled with a string tag containing all related information and packed in a heavy paper envelope.
- Rifle or shotgun – must be collected using surgical gloves and handled by the trigger guard edge and the serrated parts of the stock and forepiece; must be marked with initials in an inconspicuous place on the frame, removable parts should not be marked; must be labeled with a string tag containing all related information and packed in a heavy paper envelope.

Collecting, marking, and packing arson or fire evidence

The following are the guidelines for collecting, marking, and packing arson or fire evidence:

Copyright © Mometrix Media. You have been licensed one copy of this document for personal use only. Any other reproduction or redistribution is strictly prohibited. All rights reserved.

- Liquids – must be left in original container which should be examined for fingerprints and then must be removed from original container; must be marked with a label placed on outside of original container or proper container and label must contain location, date, time, complaint number, officer's identification; must be packed in a four ounce metal container secured with a masking tape signed by the officer.
- Ashes and other debris – must be collected with tweezers with taped ends or brushed onto heavy paper; must be marked with a label placed on outside of original container or proper container and label must contain location, date, time, complaint number, officer's identification; must be packed in a sealed clean and dry container.

Collecting, marking, and packing drug evidence

The following are the guidelines for collecting, marking, and packing drug evidence:
- Liquids – must be left in original container which should be examined for fingerprints; must be marked with a label placed on outside of original container; glass containers must be packed in absorbent material and labeled "fragile."
- Tablets – must be collected with tweezers with taped ends; must be labeled outside the container; must be packed in a sealed container or pillbox.
- Powder – must be brushed into the proper container; must be labeled outside the container; must be packed in a sealed container or pillbox.

- Solids – must be collected with tweezers with taped ends or brushed into the proper container; must be labeled outside the container; must be packed in a sealed container or pillbox.

Collecting, marking, and packing glass evidence

The following are the guidelines for collecting, marking, and packing glass evidence:
- Fragments – must be collected by the edge of larger pieces, flat surfaces must not be touched, smudges must not be removed, surfaces must be checked for latent prints; each piece must be packed in cotton or soft tissue paper and placed in a proper container labeled "fragile;" container must be marked with all related information, such as location, date, time, complaint number, officer's identification.
- Particles – must be collected with tweezers with taped ends or brushed onto heavy paper; must be packed in cotton or soft tissue paper and placed in a proper container labeled "fragile;" container must be marked with all related information, such as location, date, time, complaint number, officer's identification.

Collecting, marking, and packing contaminated clothing evidence

The following are the guidelines for collecting, marking, and packing contaminated clothing evidence:
- Collection – contaminated clothing must be collected with care in order to not lose any trace materials, including debris, blood, hair, fibers, powder burns, semen, etc.

Copyright © Mometrix Media. You have been licensed one copy of this document for personal use only. Any other reproduction or redistribution is strictly prohibited. All rights reserved.

- Marking – clothing must be marked with a string tag containing all related information, such as location, date, time, complaint number, description, officer's identification.
- Packing – garments must be packed only when dry; contaminated parts must not be cut through; each item of clothing must be wrapped in individual dry plastic evidence bags that should be labeled with information related to the crime, such as location, date, time, complaint number, officer's identification.

Collecting, marking, and packing tool and tool marks evidence

The following are the guidelines for collecting, marking, and packing tool and tool marks evidence:
- Tools – must be examined for latent prints first, then collected by the side of the tool; must be marked with initials on the side of the tool, faces and removable parts of tools must not be marked, string tags containing crime information must be attached to the tool; must be packed in an evidence bag of appropriate size.
- Tool marks – must be covered with soft tissue paper in order not to damage the mark; objects containing tool marks must be marked with initials after being transported to the laboratory, tool marks themselves must not be marked; objects containing tool marks must be secured in appropriate containers to avoid contamination, alteration, and loss.

Fingerprints

A fingerprint is a unique imprint of a person's finger containing skin oils, perspiration, and other substances. Fingerprints serve as one of the most conclusive methods in determining identity. The following are the most common techniques for lifting fingerprints:
- Dusting – the surface is dusted with black powder to develop the print; the print is photographed and lifted from the surface with adhesive tape; the imprint is placed on a white card and classified by a technician.
- Photonics – surfaces are exposed to the source of light and a polarized filter; images are taken with a digital camera and processed through a computer. The differences in fluorescent reflection are used to detect even latent fingerprints and separate them from the background noise.
- Super glue – the surface is exposed to super glue fumes; next, it is rinsed with a fluorescent dye; then, the image is taken using blue or green illumination.

Rule 803 of the Federal Rules of Evidence

Rule 803 of the Federal Rules of Evidence excludes a number of types of evidence from the hearsay thus permitting to use these types of evidence in court. The following are some of the exceptions from hearsay:
- Present sense impression
- Excited utterance
- Then existing mental, emotional, or physical condition
- Statements for purposes of medical diagnosis or treatment
- Recorded recollection

Copyright © Mometrix Media. You have been licensed one copy of this document for personal use only. Any other reproduction or redistribution is strictly prohibited. All rights reserved.

- Records of regularly conducted activity
- Absence of entry in records kept in accordance with the provisions of paragraph (6), evidence of a missing record
- Public records and reports
- Records of vital statistics
- Absence of public record or entry
- Records of religious organizations
- Marriage, baptismal, and similar certificates
- Family records
- Records of documents affecting an interest in property

Outdoors
- Recently disturbed ground
- Sawdust
- Electric wire
- Fishing line
- Rope
- Tinfoil
- String
- Abandoned vehicles
- Military containers of ammunition or explosives
- Disturbed vegetation
- Tree marks
- Footprints

Discovery in civil cases

Discovery is a legal pre-trial procedure that allows the legal representatives of both sides to familiarize themselves with the opposing party's case and prepare for their positions at trial. The following are the forms of discovery in civil cases:
- Deposition – officially recorded questioning of one party's witness by the attorney of the opposing party. Deposition may be conducted by the opposing party attorney or in presence of both attorneys.
- Interrogatory – a list of questions prepared by one party's attorney for the opposing party's witness. If the

- Statements in documents affecting an interest in property
- Statements in ancient documents
- Market reports, commercial publications.

Presence of explosives

The preliminary examination of the bomb search scene demands great concentration on physical evidence because of the danger of the operation. The following clues indicate the presence of concealed explosive devices:

Indoors
- Fresh plaster, brick, or cement
- Raised carpeting or tiles
- Loose floorboards
- Loose electrical fittings
- Greasy paper wrappings
- Out of place objects
- Half-open closets and drawers
- Ammunition
- Explosive containers
- Footprints
- Wall marks.

questions are not answered, the witness may be cited for contempt.
- Production of evidence – the legal representative of the party may request the examination of the evidence collected by the investigator of the opposing party. If the other party does not produce the evidence, the opposing party may compel the use of evidence by using a subpoena.

Copyright © Mometrix Media. You have been licensed one copy of this document for personal use only. Any other reproduction or redistribution is strictly prohibited. All rights reserved.

Conducting Interviews

Interview

An interview can be defined as a conversation between an investigator and a witness or a suspect that takes place in order to elicit information related to the current investigation. Interviews are crucial for the investigation because witnesses are usually the primary sources of information and can reveal much more than a crime scene search. The purpose of an interview is to obtain enough information to continue and possibly close the investigation. While it is important for the investigator to do everything possible to obtain information, a witness or a suspect has the legal right to remain silent; and the investigator must not threaten or intimidate the witness/suspect in any way to elicit information.

<u>Stages</u>
The stages of an interview are as follows:
- Approach – greeting the subject and presenting credentials. The investigator should try to instill a feeling of comfort and trust. The first name basis should be suggested during this stage to prepare the subject for the next stage.
- Warm-Up – the investigator should establish rapport at this stage by making conversation about some neutral topic of common interest. The investigator should express genuine interest and understanding towards the subject.
- Start – beginning of the actual interview by asking the subject to tell everything they know about the incident. The subject should not be interrupted at this stage.
- Direct questioning – asking the subject direct questions in order to clarify, add to, or reconcile inconsistencies in the original story.

- Ending – completing the interview by summarizing the subject's statements and expressing sincere gratitude for the subject's cooperation and effort.

<u>Types</u>
The types of interviews are as follows:
- Witness interview – questioning of individuals who may have seen or heard something related to the crime. Witnesses should be interviewed as soon as possible to record accurate information.
- Suspect interview – questioning of an individual who is suspected to have committed or been involved in the crime. Because of the suspected guilt or involvement, special techniques are used during the interview.
- Victim interview – questioning of an individual who has suffered from physical or emotional injuries. During this type of interview, the investigator should display empathy, concern, and compassion for the victim.
- Informant interview – questioning of an individual who possesses special information about the crime, or suspicious activity. The investigator must make all efforts to keep the informant's identity confidential.
- Ordinary citizen interview – questioning of individuals who are not involved in the crime but may possess information about witnesses, suspects, and victims of the crime.

Interview Code of Ethics

The principles of the Interview Code of Ethics are as follows:
- Verify and report the truth fairly, objectively, and impartially.
- Do not make false claims in regards to personal qualifications.
- Maintain professional, moral, and ethical conduct.
- Treat all subjects with respect.

Copyright © Mometrix Media. You have been licensed one copy of this document for personal use only. Any other reproduction or redistribution is strictly prohibited. All rights reserved.

- Do not use unethical methods, such as deception, coercion, and intimate relationships to obtain information.
- Use laws of equity and justice in application to all duties.
- Be unbiased and unprejudiced to representatives of any racial, religious, ethnic, handicap, political, or any other social group.
- Do not accept illegal or improper compensation.
- Do not engage in representation of conflicting parties.
- Avoid using slander or libel in public criticism of law enforcement, profession, agencies, and officers.

Successful interviews

Successful interviews should be conducted based on the following guidelines:
- Human needs of the subjects should be considered.
- Subjects should be treated with respect.
- Flexible methods should be applied to different subjects.
- Imagination should be used to lead the investigator through the interview.
- No judgment should be passed on the subjects.
- Personal values and opinions should not be shared.
- Positive attitude should be maintained.
- Emotions should be concealed.
- Observation, evaluation, and assessment techniques should be used to properly attend to and understand the subject's statements.
- Change of pace should be used when appropriate.
- Various types of questions should be used to obtain the fullest account of events possible.
- Trial balloon questions should be handled.

- It should always be assumed that more information could be obtained.

Interview location and comfort

Most people feel apprehensive during investigative interviews; this feeling prevents them from remembering small but important details and sharing their concerns and impressions. Also, many people feel intimidated in the presence of an investigator and might not be willing to share all the facts. Therefore, a comfortable place must be chosen for an interview to make the subject feel as relaxed as possible. The relaxed atmosphere will allow the subject to act naturally thus giving the investigator a chance to collect more accurate information. If the subject to be questioned is a victim who has been physically injured or emotionally traumatized, the investigator should allow time for medical assistance and emotional recuperation.

It is important that the location and surroundings of the interview should be comfortable for the subject. It is best to choose a familiar setting so that the subject can feel relaxed. The following are some of the requirements for conducting interviews:
- The suspect should be interviewed by only one investigator.
- If the subject is female, a woman should oversee the interview.
- The door to the interview room should not be locked.
- The furniture in the interview room should not block or hinder the subject's exit.
- The subject should be seated so that the investigator can observe his/her body movements.
- The distance between the subject and the investigator should be moderate, but can be decreased if the investigator has to console the subject.

Copyright © Mometrix Media. You have been licensed one copy of this document for personal use only. Any other reproduction or redistribution is strictly prohibited. All rights reserved.

Questions to elicit information

The following are the types of questions that are used to elicit information during an interview:

- Pointed questions – used to get a reaction from the suspect. For example, in a car accident case, the investigator might ask "How often do you drive over the speed limit?"
- Indirect questions – used to elicit the subject's thoughts, needs, feelings, and values. For example, in a workplace fraud case the investigator might say, "Many employees believe the manager is involved in the fraud. What do you think?"
- Self-appraisal questions – used to encourage the subject to identify with the person who committed a crime. For example, in an employee theft case, the investigator might ask "You have access to the inventory room, have you ever thought how easy it might be to steal something without being caught?"

Direct questioning

Direct questioning techniques are as follows:

- Ask one question at a time. This helps the subject concentrate the efforts on recollecting a specific fact or detail and gives him/her time to gather his/her thoughts.
- Ask open-ended questions. The investigator can obtain much more information because the subject is encouraged to offer explanations and reflections.
- Do not ask leading questions. The investigator should not alter the subject's account of events, therefore questions containing opinions or other suggestions should be avoided.
- Ask simple questions. Confusing questions intimidate the subject preventing him/her from giving accurate recollections and sharing all the facts.
- Encourage the subject to speak. The investigator should display genuine attention and interest in the subject's answers. This helps the subject to relax and share more information.
- Speak the same language with the subject. This helps build rapport with the subject and makes him/her feel relaxed and understood.

Questions to encourage cooperation

The following are the types of questions that encourage cooperation during an interview:

- Reflective questions – used to address objections from the subject, remove obstacles for cooperation. For example, "Let me make sure I understand this ..." (repeat the subject's statement).
- Directive questions – used to display the advantages of cooperation to the subject. For example, "You want to know why this happened, don't you?"
- Diversion questions – used to distract the subject's attention from the real questions and to build rapport between the investigator and the subject. For example, "How long have you worked for this company?"
- Leading questions – encourage cooperation when used properly. Poorly formulated leading questions should be avoided. For example, "You have been under a lot of stress lately, haven't you?" is a well formulated question. "You would like to have extra money to support your expensive hobby, wouldn't you?" is a poorly formulated question.

Trial balloon questions

"Trial balloon" is a term that refers to the questions asked by subjects in order to test their statements for consequences. For example, a subject might ask "What's the

Copyright © Mometrix Media. You have been licensed one copy of this document for personal use only. Any other reproduction or redistribution is strictly prohibited. All rights reserved.

usual punishment for this type of fraud?" or "What happens to employees caught stealing merchandise?" These questions should be handled as the first indication of the subject's readiness to make a confession. However, the investigator should not treat these questions as an admission and not display signs of excitement at the possibility of obtaining a confession. Instead, the investigator should give a calm response to the question and continue encouraging the subject to tell the truth. At this point, the investigator should exercise persistence and patience in order not to avert the subject from confessing.

Listening

Listening is a very important skill that plays a crucial role in the process and outcome of an interview. Listening carefully means understanding the real meaning of the message even if it was concealed. Listening as a communication process has four steps: receiving, attending, meaning, and remembering. The receiving step requires the interviewer's physical perception of the communicated verbal or non-verbal message. The attending step requires the interviewer's conscious control over the distractions, such as outside noise, physical appearance of the subject, the interviewer's emotions, etc., during the whole process of listening. The meaning step requires the interviewer to construct the meaning of the received verbal or non-verbal message. During this step, most of the mental analysis and interpretation occurs. The remembering step requires the interviewer to store the information for later use. The interviewer may use some memory techniques to memorize the content of the received message.

Workplace investigation interviews

Interviews should be conducted in the workplace. The following individuals might be interviewed depending on how an employee's misconduct was discovered:

- The employee accused of a fraudulent behavior
- The employee(s) who complained or was the victim of the fraud
- The customer(s) who complained or was the victim of the fraud
- The supervisor who became suspicious about an unusual activity
- The witnesses, other employees, or customers who may have seen or heard something related to the investigation.

Before setting up an interview, the investigator should prepare a list of questions in order to get as much information as possible. Open-ended questions are recommended to obtain a full account of events. The questions should allow the interviewees to tell the story in their own words. To avoid bias and protect the privacy of the subjects, the investigator must not reveal his/her opinions or the opinions of other interviewees.

Canvass technique

Canvass is the search of the area of the crime for potential witnesses. Canvass includes visiting people's homes, businesses, and public places, questioning everyone who may have heard or seen anything related to the crime. If a person was not available for the initial questioning, re-canvass must be conducted. In serious criminal cases, re-canvass is conducted multiple times in order to obtain as much information as possible. Upon the completion of questioning, the canvass report must be compiled. The report should contain date and time of the crime or incident, description of the crime/incident, description of the area that was canvassed, name of the investigator, addresses and names of all persons questioned, and results of canvass.

Written statements

A written statement must be taken after the interview with each suspect or witness. The

Copyright © Mometrix Media. You have been licensed one copy of this document for personal use only. Any other reproduction or redistribution is strictly prohibited. All rights reserved.

statements may be documented in the following ways: handwritten by the subject, dictated to a secretary and typed, tape-recorded and transcribed, or written by the investigator based on the subject's oral statements and signed by the subject. The statement should contain the following:

- Case number
- Date and time of the incident
- Location of the incident
- Name, age, date of birth, address, and telephone number of the subject
- Detailed account of events in the subject's own words
- Date and time of the interview
- Location of the interview
- Name of the investigator conducting the interview
- Number of pages in the present statement
- Names of witnesses to the statement
- Signature of the subject giving the statement.

Oral statements

An oral statement is a statement by a witness, a suspect, or any other person involved in the investigation made without written documentation. An oral statement can be recorded with the help of any audio recording device and reproduced during the hearing. In order for the oral statement to be admissible in court, the following requirements must be met:

- The investigator must prove that the statement was completely voluntary and was not obtained by means of coercion.
- The tape used to record the statement should not contain any other recordings.
- The tape should be kept on during the whole interview.
- The tape should be held secure as evidence.

Narrative statements

A narrative statement is a statement by a witness, a suspect, or any other person involved in the investigation that is recorded in written documentation. Narrative statements allow the subject to give a detailed account of events in his/her own language. The narrative statement must be hand-written, typed, or transcribed by a stenographer. In order for the narrative statement to be admissible in court, the following requirements must be met:

- There should be no corrections in the statement
- The statement should be signed by the subject and the investigator
- If the statement is made in a foreign language, a certified translation must be provided
- The statement should be accompanied by the headings containing the subject's name, the investigator's name, and the subject's contact information.

Question and answer statements

A question and answer statement is a series of questions prepared by the investigator concerning the crime or incident and the subject's responses to these questions. The first few questions should ask for identification information. The rest of the questions should be arranged in the logical and chronological order, that is, cover the events before, during, and after the crime or incident. In order for the question and answer statement to be admissible in court, the following requirements must be met:

- Investigator's name and case number should appear on the statement
- Questions should be open-ended in order to give the subject an opportunity to recollect the events in his/her own words
- Questions should not ask the subject to provide opinions or judgments.

Copyright © Mometrix Media. You have been licensed one copy of this document for personal use only. Any other reproduction or redistribution is strictly prohibited. All rights reserved.

Statement format

The following are the elements of the statement format:

- Heading – starts with the confirmation that the subject is fully aware that the statement is given voluntary and no coercion is applied; continues with the subject's personal data, such as name, date and place of birth, address, marital status, education; ends with the information on the incident, such as type of incident, date, time, location, and description of the incident, and introduction of all the parties.
- Body – contains the accurate chronological account of events seen, heard, and recollected by the subject. If the statement is obtained in a question and answer method, the exact questions and responses must be provided in the body.
- Ending – contains the hand-written acknowledgement of the subject verifying the present statement. Signatures of the subject, the investigator, and witnesses should be placed here. Corrections should be authorized by the subject's initials.

Body language

Body language can convey much more than words, therefore it is important for the investigator to pay attention to the subject's face and body movements. The following face and body signs indicate potential deception by manifesting certain emotions:

- Leaning forward, chin up manifest stubbornness and aggressiveness.
- Chin down manifests depression and remorse.
- Eyebrows squeezed together, frowning manifest confusion and anger.
- Darting eyes manifest confusion, search for an answer.

- Break of eye contact manifests remorse and tension.
- Dilated pupils manifest emotional arousal.
- Closed eyes manifest desire to escape.
- Frequent blinking manifests nervousness.
- Narrowed eyes manifest feelings of premonition.
- Hands covering eyes manifest desire to escape.
- Hands covering mouth demonstrate an urge to stop oneself from speaking.
- Hands touching nose or chin manifest tension and hesitation.
- Feet under the chair manifest desire to hide.

Symptoms of deception

Physiological
Some of the subjects may experience physiological symptoms while giving lies in response to the investigator's questions. These symptoms may include lightheadedness and numbness in the hands and feet due to the reduced blood circulation. Some subjects may display signs of high blood pressure and body temperature. These symptoms may be explained by the liar's feeling of stress and helplessness. Some other physiological symptoms of deception include such nervous reactions as burping, sweating, stuttering, crying, blinking, tics, muscular contractions. In extreme cases, lying may cause the subjects to suffer from severe headaches and regurgitation. In contrast, subjects who are telling the truth do not usually undergo stress and do not display noticeable physiological symptoms.

Verbal
The following are the verbal signs of deception that can be detected during an interview or interrogation:

- Complicated and confusing explanations – stories with many details that are often inconsistent.

Copyright © Mometrix Media. You have been licensed one copy of this document for personal use only. Any other reproduction or redistribution is strictly prohibited. All rights reserved.

- Sophisticated methods of evasion – changing the subject, speaking in general terms, avoiding questions.
- Calm manner of speaking – an assumption on the part of the subject that a composed person must be perceived as truthful.
- Signs of calculated answers – the subject takes time thinking before answering a question.
- Failure to remember – the subject confesses that he/she does not remember all the details while speaking only in general terms.
- Distraction – the subject may try to avoid questions with inappropriate behavior, such as sexual advances, compliments.
- Overuse of "truth" vocabulary – the subject's speech is abundant with words like "honestly," "truthfully," "frankly".
- Overuse of objections – the subject is not only denying the accusations, but also provides explanations.

Pathological liars

The main sign of a pathological liar is that he/she is telling lies that are exaggerated and extraordinary to the point of suggesting a mental disorder. A pathological liar makes up stories even in cases when it is easier to tell the truth. A pathological liar may sound very convincing as he/she has had a lot of experience telling lies. He/she may attempt to refute the investigator's notes denying his/her recent statements. The stories a pathological liar fabricates are very elaborate with a lot of minute details; the liar usually has the story prepared but also embellishes it as he/she proceeds. However, if asked to repeat the story, a pathological liar cannot repeat it word for word, but tells another lie that contradicts the first. A pathological liar is very defensive when accused of lying and usually manufactures some extraordinary excuses.

Methods of obtaining confessions

Lies
Only lies that exaggerate the strength of evidence and do not interfere with the suspect's free choice are permitted to obtain a confession. For example, it is allowed to tell a suspect that a witness has seen his/her vehicle near the crime scene, to tell a suspect that he/she was identified by a witness, or to tell a suspect that his/her fingerprints or other exemplars were found at the crime scene. It is not permitted to fabricate tangible or documentary evidence pointing to a suspect. For example, it is not allowed to show the suspect false lab reports proving that his/her blood was found on the victim or at the crime scene.

Threats
Threats are usually viewed in court as inherent contributors to a coercive environment. The following types of threats are not permissible for the purpose of obtaining a confession:
- Use of physical violence against the suspect.
- Threat of physical violence against the suspect.
- Threat of physical violence against the suspect's family member, relative, friend, or partner.
- Use or threat of physical violence against the defendant's co-arrestee.
- Threat of interference with normal family relationships.
- Threat to take any type of legal measures, such as deprivation of property, financial assistance, or rights, against the defendant's family members.
- Threat to separate mother defendants from their young children for a long time.

Promises
Although it is not allowed to promise leniency, suggestions of hope are considered

Copyright © Mometrix Media. You have been licensed one copy of this document for personal use only. Any other reproduction or redistribution is strictly prohibited. All rights reserved.

permissible. The following uses of promises do not render confessions involuntary:

- Promise the defendant that in exchange for a confession the investigator will inform the U.S. Attorney Office of his/her cooperation with a chance of a better treatment. The investigator should make sure that he/she does not guarantee the reduction of the sentence.
- Promise to release the suspect's family member, friend, partner, or relative who was being held in police custody.
- Promise to provide psychological counseling.
- Promise to provide drug addiction treatment.
- Promise to provide alcohol addiction treatment.
- Promise to provide rape counseling.

Self-fulfilling prophesy

The self-fulfilling prophecy is a term that refers to the concept that expectation produces the reality. In practice, it means that if an investigator expects and visualizes the suspect's confession, he/she is more likely to obtain it than another investigator who did not expect a confession. The self-fulfilling prophecy applied to interrogations is made up of two kinds of expectations. The first is the expectations of the investigator of him/herself. It implies the investigator's high belief in his/her talents and capability to achieve the desired goal. The second is the expectations from the suspect. It implies the investigator's belief in the suspect's guilt and facilitates his/her attitude during the interrogation. The attitude, however, should always be positive and non-judgmental. Both beliefs on the investigator's part influence his/her behavior during the interrogation thus securing success in obtaining a confession.

The following are the four elements of the self-fulfilling prophesy:

- Climate – can be positive or negative; is created through mannerisms, eye contact, facial expressions, gestures, posture, tone of voice, silence; sets the stage for the interview by using the subject's fears or moral values to encourage cooperation.
- Feedback – the process of adjusting the subsequent actions based on the received results of the previous communication. Well-prepared investigators can predict subjects' reactions to their behavior and take control over the interview's results.
- Input – verbal and non-verbal messages that convey the investigator's expectations. The input should be planned ahead in order not to give the subject a chance to surprise or distract the investigator.
- Output – the subject's response to the investigator's communicated expectations. Carefully planned input produces the desired output. Positive humane attitude displayed in the investigator's verbal and non-verbal messages encourages the subject's to tell the truth.

Legal tactics

The following are the legal tactics used to obtain a confession during an interrogation:

- The investigator's behavior should display certainty in the suspect's guilt.
- The investigator should be ready to present circumstantial evidence to convince the subject to confess.
- The investigator should vigilantly observe the suspect's behavior for verbal and non-verbal signs of deception.
- The investigator should display empathy with the suspect and help him/her to explain his/her actions to save face.

Copyright © Mometrix Media. You have been licensed one copy of this document for personal use only. Any other reproduction or redistribution is strictly prohibited. All rights reserved.

- The investigator should not emphasize the graveness of the matter, but make every effort to minimize it in order not to scare the suspect from giving a confession.
- The investigator should not judge the suspect's behavior but merely accept it.
- The investigator should demonstrate that it would be in the suspect's interests to confess.

Special tactics

Although the introduction of Miranda rights sequestered many of the police tactics for obtaining confessions from suspects, some of them, including lies, promises, and threats, are still used. The legality of these tactics is determined by the court's examination of all the attendant's circumstances on a case-by-case basis. If it is found that overreaching, intimidation, or coercion was used to obtain a confession, the confession is considered a breach of the Fourth Amendment rights and thus inadmissible in court. However, use of special tactics does not always translate into inadmissibility of the confession. The totality-of-circumstances test determines if the confession was given voluntarily. Therefore, some deception may be used lawfully in order to obtain a confession as long as Miranda rights are not violated.

Miranda ruling

The court rule on the Miranda vs. Arizona case decided that all confessions are coercive by nature, and thus any confession obtained during police custody is not voluntary. The Court ruled that the interrogations violated the Fourth Amendment and established the so-called Miranda warnings which were to be applied to any interrogation. Since then, investigators were obligated by law to do the following prior to the start of an interview:
- Inform the suspect that he/she has the right to remain silent.

- Inform the suspect that anything he/she says may be used in court against him/her.
- Inform the suspect that he/she has the right to contact his/her attorney and request the attorney's presence during the interview.
- Inform the suspect that he/she has the right to an attorney whose services will be free of charge.

Fifth Amendment

The Fifth Amendment protects the subject's right to remain silent. It guarantees that "no person shall be held to answer for a capital, or otherwise infamous crime, unless on a presentment or indictment of a Grand Jury," except in specified cases; and no person "shall be compelled in any criminal case to be a witness against himself." The subsequent court rulings based on the Fifth Amendment prohibit coercion and intimidation as means of obtaining an admission or confession. Any investigator who has been observed to use coercion or failed to inform the subject of his/her right to remain silent is considered a violator of the constitutional right and a subject to lawful prosecution.

Intensity of review and encouragement

The intensity of the review and encouragement, which may vary throughout the stages of the interview, can influence the subject's inclination to tell the truth. The Level 1 and 2 intensity employs general review and minimal encouragement and is aimed at clarification of certain details and informing the subject of the implications of lying. The Level 3 and 4 intensity employs review of specific details and more determined encouragement. At these levels, the investigator points out the specific inconsistencies in the subject's statement and attempts to persuade him/her to reveal the truth voluntarily. The Level 5 intensity uses the same specific review and determined encouragement as Level 4, but the

Copyright © Mometrix Media. You have been licensed one copy of this document for personal use only. Any other reproduction or redistribution is strictly prohibited. All rights reserved.

investigator exhibits a stronger belief in the subject's deception and makes a greater effort to convince the subject to give a voluntary confession.

Polygraph

Polygraph, or the lie detector, is a mechanical device that takes body measurements, such as pulse, blood pressure, temperature, breathing rate, and skin conductivity, to determine if the subject is lying. The use of polygraph for obtaining information is based on the belief that lying is combined with stress which manifests itself in certain body reactions. A polygraph can be used to confirm subjects' statements, verify information provided by other subjects, direct the investigation, and obtain a confession. Suspects who have been subjected to a polygraph test may choose to make a confession when notified that they failed the test, or they may confess as soon as they are notified of the imminent test.

<u>Restrictions in workplace investigations</u>
By the Federal Polygraph Protection Act, polygraph testing is legally restricted to pre-employment screening for government positions. It means that only certain governmental agencies are permitted to use the polygraph testing to screen applicants. In some cases, the use of polygraph testing is permitted during an ongoing workplace investigation. These cases include investigations involving economic loss, such as loss of property or assets, or serious damage to the company's business, such as discredit. There must be proof that the employee to be subjected to test had access to the lost property or was involved in activities damaging to the company's business. In all other cases, the use of polygraph testing is prohibited unless the suspected employee gives consent to be tested.

Invasion of privacy

<u>Legality</u>
Four considerations that determine the legality of the invasion of privacy in a workplace investigation are as follows:
- Consideration of the zones of privacy. The highest zone is the person's clothing, immediate possessions, such as briefcases, purses, backpacks, vehicles. The medium zone is the person's immediate work area, such as the desk, the cubicle, the office. The lowest zone is the larger work area, including the floor, the building, and the parking lot.
- Consideration of the risks. The higher the zone of privacy, the higher the risk is of illegal invasion of privacy. The highest zones imply the highest expectations of privacy.
- Consideration of the reasons for invading privacy. The more compelling the evidence is, the more reasons the investigator has to invade even the highest zone of privacy.
- Consideration of the need for surveillance. If the employer's need to observe the suspected employee's behavior outweighs the reasonable expectation of privacy, invasion of privacy is legally justified.

<u>Theories</u>
The following are four theories related to the invasion of privacy:
- Public Disclosure of a Person's Private Life – this theory is based on the Fourth Amendment. In case the investigator releases information offensive to the public or not of the public's concern, he/she may be accused of violating the privacy right.
- Placing in False Light – this theory is based on the premise that any information published must be true. If the investigator releases information that presents the subject in a false

Copyright © Mometrix Media. You have been licensed one copy of this document for personal use only.
Any other reproduction or redistribution is strictly prohibited. All rights reserved.

light, positive or negative, he/she may be held liable.

- Intrusion into a Person's Seclusion – this theory is based on the premise that every person has a right to a reasonable physical and psychological space. If the investigator violates this space, he/she may be held liable.
- Intentional Infliction of Emotional Stress – the investigator is prohibited from abusing the subject physically or verbally in order not to cause emotional distress. The investigator must not accuse the subject of dishonesty or crime.

Copyright © Mometrix Media. You have been licensed one copy of this document for personal use only. Any other reproduction or redistribution is strictly prohibited. All rights reserved.

Conducting Research

Competitive intelligence acquisition

Competitive intelligence acquisition is a process of collecting, interpreting, and distributing publicly held information that is essential for the investigation. The process consists of the following steps:

- Selection (determining intelligence needs and choosing the sources)
- Collection (obtaining information)
- Interpretation (analyzing and verifying data, and determining subsequent actions)
- Distribution (disseminating findings)

Information must be obtained legally and ethically through open sources, such as officially published documents, news and scholarly publications, court transcripts, libraries, public records, voluntary interviews, authorized onsite observations, web pages open for public access. Information must not be obtained through covert surveillance, disguised radio transmitters, communication intercepts, and other clandestine illegal or unethical methods.

Electronic sources and search engines

Electronic sources are any sources of information that exist only in electronic form, such as a computer file, database, or web page. The Internet is the most accessible electronic source that can instantly provide and sort a large amount of data. To conduct successful Internet research, one must know how to use a search engine. The following are the general rules for using a search engine:

- Choose a search engine that suits your needs best. Answers.com is best for commercial information, Google Beta is better for academic information, Yahoo People Search is best for finding personal data.
- Use a URL restriction option to limit the search to websites with specific URL, such as gov., edu., or org.
- Use quotation marks around the key words to ensure that the search engine only displays results with these words.
- Use Boolean operators, that is, the words AND, OR, and NOT to narrow down your search.

Physical sources

Physical sources can be defined as any tangible sources of information such as printed documents, published public records, books and encyclopedias, magazines, etc. The credibility of the sources can be determined by identifying the author, publisher, existing bias, currency and relevance of information. Based on these criteria, the following physical sources are considered credible and can be used to obtain information:

- Documents published by the government – all types of records, regulatory acts, legislative documents, and registries.
- Legal documents – legal files, cases, proceedings, and letters.
- Documents published by federal agencies, such as FDA, USDA, DOD, HHS, and FERC.
- Scientific records – any documents issued by a scientific agency, or a scientific publication.
- Public education records – student records, grade books, and student and teacher biographies.
- Encyclopedias – Encyclopedia Britannica, the ADAM Medical Encyclopedia, etc.

Electronic people finders

People finders are websites which serve as directories for locating individuals by name, address, phone number, and other data. Most of the large search engines, such as Yahoo, Lycos, AOL, etc. have phone directories, white

Copyright © Mometrix Media. You have been licensed one copy of this document for personal use only. Any other reproduction or redistribution is strictly prohibited. All rights reserved.

and yellow pages. There are a number of independent comprehensive people search engines, such as PeopleFinders.com, Addresses.com, USA-People-Search.com, Infospace.com, Anywho.com, Locateme.com, etc. The sites provide initial search for free but charge for reports. For example, at PeopleFinders.com it is possible to conduct a people search, background check, criminal check, property search, marriage, divorce, and death records search. The initial search brings a list of records indicated as available, and then there is a possibility to purchase a record. The databases of these sites are based on existing phone books and address listings; therefore, if the person's phone number or address is not listed it is impossible to find this person through these websites.

Internet

Some of the advantages of using the Internet for investigative research are:
- Accessibility
- Availability of large amounts of data
- Availability of information sorting and categorizing option
- Availability of information free of charge
- Speed
- An option to save or print the data
- An option to quickly transport and share data.

Some of the disadvantages of using the Internet for investigative research are:
- Difficulty in narrowing down the search results
- Inability to verify information
- Unavailability of publisher's information
- Presentation of information from a biased point of view
- Inability to check the currency of information
- Potential risk to be identified as a site visitor.

State government sources

The following are the types of state government sources and documents available from them:
- Attorney General – records documenting efforts in the areas of criminal justice, civil enforcement, and consumer protection; functions as the state office in charge of these areas.
- Bureau of Vital Statistics – birth, marriage, and death certificates, adoption papers.
- Department of Motor Vehicles – information of driver's license issuance, vehicle registrations, titles, transfers, sales, emission inspection reports, copies of photographs.
- Regulatory Agencies, such as Bureau of Professional and Vocational Standards of Department of Licensing, Controller/Treasurer, Department of Agriculture, Department of Industrial Relations, Department of Natural Resources, Gambling Commission/Horse Racing Board, Secretary Of State, Department of Corrections, Liquor Commissions, Lottery Commissions, Securities Commissions, Utility Commissions – various activity licenses, operation permits, and tax information.

Local government sources

The following are the types of local government sources and documents available from them:
- Building Inspector – blueprints, plans, permits, inspection reports.
- Coroner/Medial Examiner - coroner register.
- Court Clerk – civil court files, depositions, divorce complaints, probate indexes.

Copyright © Mometrix Media. You have been licensed one copy of this document for personal use only. Any other reproduction or redistribution is strictly prohibited. All rights reserved.

- Health Department – death certificates, property inspection reports, local health problems reports.
- Human Resources Department – employment histories, efficiency reports, disciplinary acts records, salary histories.
- Public Schools – student records, grade books, student and teacher biographies.
- Recorder's Offices – real estate transactions, mortgages, wills, official bonds, bankruptcy papers, veteran status papers, marriage licenses and certificates.
- Registrar of Voters – affidavit of registration with personal and demographic information.
- Regulatory Agencies – applications for business licenses.
- Surveyor – maps of evaluations, rights of way, easement, etc.
- Tax Assessor – maps of real property.

Informants

An informant is a motivated individual who voluntarily provides information to law enforcement agencies. Some of the informant motivators include revenge, fear, attempt to avoid punishment, financial gain, moral and ethical values, and seeking social approval. The use of informants can be crucial for the investigation, and that is why the investigator should follow these general rules of dealing with informants:
- Understand the motivation behind the informant's consent to provide information. It might be important for the verification of information.
- Always treat informants with respect and never refer to them in derogatory terms.
- Always try to verify information obtained from an informant.
- Do not disclose all the facts about the investigation but only those necessary to obtain information.

- Keep the communication with the informant confidential; do not use traceable means, such as letters or cell phone conversations.
- Never make promises that cannot be kept.
- Use a third party to make contact.
- Never ask an informant to break the law.

The following groups of people can act as informants:
- Law abiding citizens who believe in exposing criminals and wrongdoers. These can be employees, neighbors, associates, anyone who agrees to provide information based on the motive of "doing the right thing."
- Individuals who are in fear of the law or law enforcement authorities. These can be persons who have committed crimes of various gravity and who wish to be protected by the law rather than prosecuted. They trade information in exchange for protection. Some other motives include revenge, financial gain, remorse, and ego.
- Individuals who may be incapacitated in some respects and who enjoy sharing information without an apparent motive. These persons are usually called gossip and their information may turn out to be rumors and assumptions.

Federal agencies

The following are federal agencies and documents available from each:
- Department of Agriculture – company contacts with the agency; records of recipients of financial benefits; data on import and export of agricultural commodities, animals, and plants; crop yield reports and business profits; plans of property; loan applications and financial statements; data on ownership, management, and

Copyright © Mometrix Media. You have been licensed one copy of this document for personal use only. Any other reproduction or redistribution is strictly prohibited. All rights reserved.

operation of farms that participate in USDA programs.

- Department of Commerce – documents on international trade, economic statistic, records of patents and trademarks.
- Department of Defense – military records such as pay, dependents, allotments, deposits, financial papers and medical histories of military personnel.
- Federal Energy Regulatory Commission – electric utility and gas company reports, license and permit information.
- Food and Drug Administration – food and drug company annual reports, license and permit information, FDA investigation reports.

Physical research for pre-employment investigations

The following research methods are used in pre-employment investigations:

- Research of military records – the applicant's copy of DD-214 should be verified against a similar record which may be obtained from the national Personnel Records Center in St. Louis, Missouri. The record should contain dates of entry and discharge from the service and all locations where the person was assigned.
- Research of educational records – the certificates and diplomas should be verified against the records which may be obtained through the educational institutions. Departments of Education provide records for the schools that are no longer open. Diplomas and certificates obtained via distance learning can be verified through Distance Education and Training Counsel.
- Research of criminal history records – can be conducted by examining public court records.

- Research of credit history records – can be conducted through examining records maintained by one of the following companies: Trans Union, Experian, or Equifax.

Access to confidential data

Although the sources of information are the same for private investigators and law enforcement agencies, private investigators have more liberty in accessing confidential records as directed by the client. Private investigators have more time and often more funds to dedicate to detailed research. Also, the purposes of a private investigation may not require the evidence to be admissible in court. However, private investigators are constrained by the Privacy of Information Act prohibiting them from accessing credit histories, banking records, government financial records, and police records. Often, telephone company records, employment history, and criminal records are restricted for private investigators. However, if the initiator of the investigation is the employer, many records may become obtainable.

Legislative acts
The following are federal legislative acts regulating access to public records:

- Privacy Act of 1974 – protects individual records maintained by an agency, such as medical history, education, and criminal history.
- Financial Privacy Act of 1978 – protects confidentiality of financial records such as bank accounts.
- Privacy Protection Act of 1980 – protects a person and his/her property from the invasion of the reasonable expectation of privacy.
- Fair Financial Information Practices Act of 1981 – protects individuals and agencies from unfair and biased financial information practices, such as concealment and distortion of financial information.

Copyright © Mometrix Media. You have been licensed one copy of this document for personal use only. Any other reproduction or redistribution is strictly prohibited. All rights reserved.

- Privacy of Electronic Fund Transfers Act of 1981 – protects the rights on confidentiality of electronic transfers.
- Fair Credit Reporting Act of 1970 – ensures fair and accurate credit reporting to agencies and individuals.
- Omnibus and Crime Control Bill of 1968 – protects crime witnesses.
- Freedom of Information Act – requires each agency to provide to the public information on the agency's organization, locations, general course and method.

The Federal Freedom of Information Act allows the public to get access to federal records and documentation. The FOIA applies to cabinet departments, military departments, government corporations and corporations controlled by the government, independent regulatory agencies, and any other agency and office within the executive branch of the federal government. The Act improves investigative research by giving the investigators a greater freedom in obtaining access to the federal records and examining federal documents. The amendments to the Act allow for the same freedom at the state and local level which means that private investigators have legitimate justification for their search for information. Any agency that received a request to look for a specific record is obliged by law to do so even if it means exposing fraudulent activity. However, the request should be as specific as possible and made in a written form.

Fairness in collection of information

In order to balance interests of the client, the subject, and the source of information, the following principles must be observed:
- Personal information systems that contain secret data should not be maintained.
- A subject must be aware of a personal information file maintained on him/her and have access to this file.
- A subject should be able to make corrections and update the personal information file.
- The personal information must be used only for the purposes for which it was collected. The subject's consent is needed to use the personal information for any other purpose.
- Personal information files should contain accurate, updated, relevant, and complete data.
- Personal information files must be protected from unauthorized access, alteration, or elimination.

Copyright © Mometrix Media. You have been licensed one copy of this document for personal use only. Any other reproduction or redistribution is strictly prohibited. All rights reserved.

Case Presentation

Official written reports

Official reports are categorized in observations, client, and supervisor reports. The following are the description of each category and type of official written reports:

- Observation – contains a detailed account of any actions witnessed by the investigator at the crime scene, during interviews, interrogations, or surveillance.
- Preliminary supervisor or client report – identifies the case, presents all the available facts and the status of the investigation; may serve as a basis for a media report.
- Progress or interim supervisor or client report – used in lengthy investigations; documents the progress of the investigation; may be submitted at pre-determined intervals or if necessity arises that calls for immediate action.
- Final supervisor or client report – completes the closed case or notifies of the impossibility to successfully close the case; includes a summary of the case history and results.

Content

Each investigative agency has its own specific guidelines for writing official reports, however, there is general content that must be included in each official report. An official written report should contain the following:

- Administrative data – date and time the report was written; case number, title and classification; names and demographic data on complainants, subjects, and investigators; status of the investigation.
- Synopsis – an executive summary of the following report presenting the brief history of the investigation.

- Details – an accurate and elaborate narrative describing each action that has been taken so far in the course of the investigation.
- Conclusions and recommendations – a summary of the report presenting the results obtained so far; recommendations to continue or close the case based on the conclusions.

Investigative report as PR tool

Since reports are a form of communication between an investigative agency and its client, reports make a great impact on the agency's image. A comprehensive dependable system of documenting and maintaining records instills a feeling of trust into the client and makes the client more determined to invest substantial funds in the investigation. Another role of reports is to educate the client on the investigative procedures and the nature of the obtained results. It is important to show the client the evidence of the agency's work in the form of action and expenditure reports. A clear concise complete report serves not only to document the investigation, but also to demonstrate to the client the agency's professionalism and competency. Reports serve as persuasive tools that help to sell the agency's services.

Report types

The following are types of reports used in private investigations:

- Incident reports – documents recording and describing the circumstances of an incident.
- Memorandum files – documents containing the record of exchanged information during an investigation.
- Expenditure reports – documents recording and describing various expenses pertaining to the investigation.
- Equipment files – documents containing data on investigative equipment.

Copyright © Mometrix Media. You have been licensed one copy of this document for personal use only. Any other reproduction or redistribution is strictly prohibited. All rights reserved.

- Personnel files – personal information files.
- Sequential documentation – logs and other documents recording the signoff.
- Intelligence reports – documents recording the collected intelligence.
- Investigative reports – initial, follow-up, and final reports documenting the process of an investigation.
- Evidence reports – documents recording and describing the evidence collected.
- Statistical files – statistical data on investigations, crimes, etc.
- Arrest reports – documents recording the detention of a suspect.
- Search report – documents recording and describing the search of a crime scene.

Report writing

The five elements of report writing are:
- Completeness – a report should cover all aspects of the investigation in detail. While reading the report, the audience, the client, or the supervisor should be able to visualize events, people, or objects described. A complete report should include negative as well as positive results.
- Conciseness – a report should cover only those details that are necessary for understanding the course of the investigation. Technicalities, complex clauses, and other cluttering elements should be omitted.
- Clearness – a report should be written in a clear language. Short descriptive sentences should be used, as well as neutral wording, correct spelling, punctuation, and grammar.
- Correctness – a report should give an accurate account of events. Opinions, biased interpretations, experiences should be omitted. Only verified factual information should be presented.

- Courteousness – a report should present information in an objective manner. The investigator should not attempt to judge anyone or express his/her subjective opinion.

The report writing process is as follows:
- Review the notes taken at the crime scene during interviews, interrogations, or surveillance.
- Make a list of facts that must be included in the report.
- Add ideas such as descriptions and details to each fact.
- Write the first draft, either by hand or using a word processor, based on the idea cluster. At this stage, focus on writing down all the facts that must be documented in the report. Do not pay attention to wording, spelling, sentence structure, punctuation, and other small things.
- Read your draft and revise it focusing on the main idea and adding details omitted in the first draft.
- Revise the second draft concentrating on the wording and structure of the report.
- Edit your report for spelling, syntax, grammar, and punctuation.
- Write an executive summary briefly presenting the report in one paragraph.

Arrest reports

Since private investigators have the same power to arrest as any citizen, they are subject to reasonable suspicion. Therefore, for the purposes of liability and record-keeping, private investigators must document their actions in an arrest report. The arrest report serves as the private investigator's protection from accusations of erroneous arrest and prosecution. The victims of arrests supported by their employers may file a lawsuit against the private investigator which may result in the loss of certification. In this case, the arrest report is the main evidence in

- 79 -

Copyright © Mometrix Media. You have been licensed one copy of this document for personal use only. Any other reproduction or redistribution is strictly prohibited. All rights reserved.

defense of the private investigator. The report should contain all the important information so that the police can take over the subsequent procedures.

The contents of the arrest report are as follows:

- Heading Block: Suspect's name, address, phone number, social security number, sex, race, gender, height, weight, color of eyes and hair, date and place of birth, occupation; complaint number; weapon serial number and description; date and time when the crime occurred and was reported; description of formal charges; and UCR classification
- Body Block: Location of arrest; description of the location; day and time of arrest; details on resistance; breathalyzer reading; details on vehicle, if involved; information on witnesses, victims, and co-suspects; duration of arrest, transportation, processing, interviewing, arraignment, commitment, implied contest law, and release; a narrative account of the arrest procedures; identification of transporting officer, arresting officer, booking officer, supervisor; officer's observations; reason for stop of vehicle; field test; and chemical test.

Report format

Reports are usually formatted so that they contain a heading, a narrative, and a conclusion. The heading appears in a pre-designed block format based on the type of investigation. For example, insurance case reports include policy number and the name of the insurer. The narrative is the body of the report and must be written in chronological order in the first person. Names should be identified at the beginning and all letters of a last name must be capital. First names appear only once at the beginning. If only the initial of the last name is available it should be

surrounded with quotation marks. Objects and persons should be described as deliberately as possible. Time should be recorded in 24-hour format. The conclusion identifies the status of the investigation and makes recommendations for further action. It should not contain the summary of the investigation.

Bomb search reports

If a private investigation agency is involved in protection and prevention of terrorism, the investigators must be prepared to write reports on search for explosives. A bomb search report may contain the following:

- Heading Block: Warnings; location and description of the area searched; location of the found suspicious object; description of the suspicious object; sketch of the object.
- Body Block: Presence of the ticking timer; smell of burning fuse; visibility of trip wires or booby traps; exact time of finding; sketch of the object's position; accessibility of the object; sketch of the route to the object; additional search results; evacuation details; presence of people near the suspicious object; count of people at site; presence of valuable objects, equipment near the suspicious object.
- Conclusion Block: Name of reporting officer; date and time.

Security department review reports

Review reports are written on a regular basis, such as weekly, monthly, and yearly in order to document and maintain the records of activities occurred during a specific period of time. The purpose of review reports is to measure efficiency and promote accountability among the agency personnel. A review report may contain the following information:

- Date and time
- Period of review

Copyright © Mometrix Media. You have been licensed one copy of this document for personal use only. Any other reproduction or redistribution is strictly prohibited. All rights reserved.

- Categories of crimes and incidents, such as theft, missing property, damage to property, equipment tampering, presence of foreign objects, concealed shortage, diversion, sabotage, crank phone calls and letters, vehicle accidents, employee problems, assault, battery, substance abuse, larceny from vehicle, warehouse and truck checks
- Identification of investigations continued and closed.

Daily reports

Daily reports are filled out to document daily activities, such as time of arrival and departure, and any actions taken throughout the day. Daily reports are most often used in security departments and should contain the following information:
- Time and date of the shift
- Officer's identification
- Time and date of arrival and departure
- Identification of the relieving officer
- Number of communication device
- Checklist for details, such as fire hazards, smoking violations, open or broken doors or windows, open or broken safes or vaults, trespassing, suspicious activity, attempted and committed thefts, property damage, parking violations, safety hazards, blocked exits, extinguished security lights
- Identification and signature of inspector
- Date and time of inspection.

Inspection reports

Inspection reports are used in civil and criminal misconduct cases and serve as standardized documentation of compliance with safety procedures and policies. An inspection report may contain the following information:
- Heading Block: District/department; address of property inspected;

classification of property inspected; date and time of inspection.
- Body Block: Condition of locks, windows, doors, gates, fences; lighting conditions; condition of entrances and exits; cable, material, tool, equipment storage conditions; communication equipment condition; fire hazards; identification of responsible employees; address of responsible department; repeated condition, if any.
- Conclusion Block: Identification of reporting officer; date of report; supervisor approval.

Missing person reports

The purpose of the missing person report is to collect as much information as possible in order to answer the public and private law enforcement concern and to possibly provide a lead for solving the case. A missing person report may contain the following:
- Heading Block: Complaint number.
- Body Block: Message key indicating disability, juvenile, endangered, involuntary, or victim; missing person's name; race, sex, age, date and place of birth; date of emancipation; height, weight, color of eyes and hair, hair description, skin tone, peculiarities; social security number; other identification numbers; fingerprint classification; operators' license details; last day of contact; blood type; details on circumcision; footprints; vision details; jewelry details; handedness; build; narrative of any other relevant information.
- Conclusion Block: Reporting officer identification; date and time; supervisor approval.

Property reports

Private investigators in retail and insurance settings are responsible for writing property

Copyright © Mometrix Media. You have been licensed one copy of this document for personal use only. Any other reproduction or redistribution is strictly prohibited. All rights reserved.

reports. The purpose of property reports is to document internal and external pilferage and to catalogue, itemize, and describe the stolen property. A property report may contain the following information:

- Heading Block: Name of victim; complaint number; victim's address, phone number, other contact information; address and date of crime; date of report.
- Body Block: Itemized description of stolen property including quantity, make, model, shape, color, size, classification, serial number, age, monetary value; victim's statement, signature, and date; victim's remarks; instructions for completing the form.
- Conclusion Block: Reporting officer identification; date of report; identification of reviewer.

Traffic reports

The agency which is entrusted with and authorized to monitor a specific area is responsible for writing regular traffic reports. Since traffic violations are frequent, a daily, weekly, or monthly log is usually maintained by the agent in charge. A traffic report may contain the following information:

- Heading Block: Period of time during which the traffic violations have been logged; date.
- Body Block: Time and date of each traffic violation; vehicle type, make, model, description, license plate or permit number of each vehicle involved; count of all vehicles involved in the traffic violation; precise location of the incident.
- Conclusion Block: Identification of reporting officer; supervisor's approval.

Offence reports

Offence reports, or general crime reports, present the first record of examination and investigation of criminal cases. These reports require many details and can be lengthy. Sometimes supplemental reports are written to conclude the main report. An offence report may contain the following information:

- Heading Block: Victim's name; complaint number; victim's address, telephone number, and other contact information; victim's race, sex, age; location, date and time of crime; identity and contact information of reporting person; date and time the crime was reported; classification of crime.
- Body Block: Details on location of crime; details on classification of crime; witnesses' names and contact information; missing persons' names and description; vehicles involved count and description; property missing count and description; narrative account.
- Concluding Block: Reporting officer's identity; status of investigation; supervisor approval; date.

Security surveys

A private investigator may be responsible for filling out a security survey if he/she is called to determine a breach of security in a business or industrial setting. The purpose of security surveys is to document the company's current security status and assist in policy making. A security survey may contain the following information:

- Heading Block: Business name, address, phone number; date of inspection.
- Body Block: Condition of doors; condition of windows; condition of key security; illumination conditions; alarm conditions; cash control; physical arrangements of the premises; condition of physical security; training of the currently employed security personnel; additional concerns.
- Conclusion Block: Identity of the agent conducting the survey; date.

Copyright © Mometrix Media. You have been licensed one copy of this document for personal use only. Any other reproduction or redistribution is strictly prohibited. All rights reserved.

Victim find notification report

The following are the most important pieces of information that should be included on the victim find notification report:

- Identification of the individual who found the victim
- Time and date of the find
- Identification of the authorities that the victim find was reported to initially
- Date of the initial report
- Condition of the victim
- Description of medical response, if any, and identification of the individual who performed it
- Identification of the medical facility performing the transportation of the victim, if applicable
- In fatal cases, the existence and content of a dying statement
- Identification of witnesses
- Identification of the victim, if possible
- Identification of the individual who identified the victim
- Cause of death or injuries
- Description of physical evidence, if any
- Identification of weapons, if possible
- Identification or description of the suspect
- Proof of the suspect's description dissemination to the media.

Traffic accident reports

The purpose of traffic accident reports is to collect as much information as possible for subsequent investigation. Many traffic accident reports look like checklists. A traffic accident report may contain the following information:

- Heading Block: Date, time, and location of accident.
- Body Block: Name and contact information on each driver; each driver's license number and state of issuance; each driver's date of birth; each vehicle owner's name and contact information; each vehicle's type, year, make, model, color; each vehicle's registration number and state; each vehicle's insurance name and address; passengers' names, dates of births and contact information; statements pertaining to the circumstances of the accident; witnesses' names, age, and contact information; injured persons' names, age, contact information; description of injuries; injured persons' insurance name and address.
- Conclusion Block: Reporting officer's identification; date.

Investigator's notes

The investigator's notes should record the following details:

- Weather conditions
- Lighting conditions
- Suspect's or victim's clothing
- Location and description of roads
- Medical personnel at the scene
- Witness, victim, and suspect statements
- Documented activities of forensic technicians, photographers, sketchers, etc.
- Addresses and phone numbers of witnesses, victims, and other important persons
- Record of alterations at the crime scene
- Exact location of the crime scene
- Description of the crime scene conditions
- Detailed descriptions of real evidence, including marks, identification, date and time, exact location, custody conditions
- Descriptions of photographs including photographer's name, time and date, setting, conditions of photography, technical details.

- 83 -

Copyright © Mometrix Media. You have been licensed one copy of this document for personal use only. Any other reproduction or redistribution is strictly prohibited. All rights reserved.

Workplace investigation report

As soon as the investigation is complete, the investigator should write a report giving a detailed explanation of the investigator's actions and rationale for these actions. The purpose of the report is not only to legally protect the company initiating the investigation, but also to provide a documented record for potential future offence by the same employee(s). The report should cover the following points:

- When and how the company discovered fraudulent behavior
- Who initiated the investigation, and when
- Who was interviewed in connection with the investigation, and when
- Detailed record of each interview
- Detailed record of other evidence and documents considered in the investigation
- Interpretations of data and conclusions
- Justification of conclusions
- Detailed record of a disciplinary or other sanction brought about by the results of the investigation.

Note taking

The following key words are used in note taking:

- "Who" may refer to the client, suspect, witness, or victim. All the information related to any of these individuals should be recorded in this category.
- "What" may refer to objectives of the investigation, crime or incident, circumstances of the crime, evidence, documents, or property.
- "Where" refers to location of the crime, place where the victim or stolen property was found, or location of a surveillance operation.
- "When" refers to time and date of the crime. The time recorded should be as specific as possible and include day, month, year, hour, and minutes. In

some cases season may also be indicated.
- "How" may refer to the manner the crime was committed, the way the victim sought protection, or the manner the future incidents may be prevented.
- "Why" refers to the motive of the crime, as well as motives of witnesses and other subjects.

<u>Styles</u>
Styles of note taking and their advantages and disadvantages are as follows:

- Narrative – a descriptive style of writing which allows the investigator to give a detailed account of events in his/her own words. The advantage of the narrative style is that it gives the investigator an opportunity to document the language used by the interviewee. The disadvantage is that the narratives may get too lengthy and time-consuming to use most of the time.
- Question and Answer – an interrogative style of note taking where questions are designed to obtain specific information. Questions may be taken from other reports or interviews, even from other investigations. The advantage of this style is that it allows collection of concrete information quickly. The disadvantage is that pre-designed questions do not allow the interviewee to recollect and share any other related information.
- Chronological – this style is used to document time related information. It is good for taking notes on anything that requires a clear timeline.

Computerized report writing

Computerized report writing systems have been recently introduced to the world of professional investigation and have proved to have many advantages over the traditional

Copyright © Mometrix Media. You have been licensed one copy of this document for personal use only. Any other reproduction or redistribution is strictly prohibited. All rights reserved.

report writing. The advantages of computerized report writing systems include:

- Significant reduction of the time spent on report writing, allowing more time for patrol and investigations.
- Improvement of legibility, accuracy, and quality of reports.
- Introduction of a standardized system for collection and dissemination of information.
- Ease and acceleration of access to centralized database.
- Provision of the public with the efficient and convenient official reporting service.
- Expedition of the investigation process by providing an effective file distribution, sorting, and analysis unit.
- Improvement of follow-up investigation procedures by providing a quick access to all the necessary documents in a short period of time.

Preformatted reports

The following are the types of preformatted reports used in case management:

- Incident reports – contain identification of victims and witnesses, details of crime or incident, identification or description of perpetrator, identification or description of property taken or damaged. Incident reports are written by the first responding officer.
- Follow-Up reports – document each action taken in the course of the investigation; contain interviews, interrogations, crime scene searches, investigative research. Follow-up reports are written by the primary investigator, although other assigned members of the investigative team contribute.
- Property reports – contain information on any property collected or seized during the investigation.

- Lab reports – written by an investigator to request lab analysis of collected evidence or written by a lab technician presenting the results of the analysis.
- Supervisory Review reports – written by the investigator's supervisor upon the review of the case; may contain recommendation to close or continue the case.

Indictment and arraignment

Indictment is a term that refers to a formal charge of having committed a serious crime. In most U.S. jurisdictions retaining the grand jury, prosecutors can obtain an indictment from a grand jury or file a charging document directly with the court. This document is usually called an accusation or complaint. In felony cases where the suspect's freedom right is at stake, a preliminary hearing takes place where a judge determines the existence of a probable cause that the suspect in custody committed the crime. Arraignment is a term that refers to the formal reading of a criminal complaint which takes place after indictment or after the preliminary hearing. Arraignment is conducted in the presence of the defendant to inform him/her of the charges against him/her. After the charges are read the accused is asked to enter a plea. If the plea is "not guilty" the trial date is set.

Entrapment

Entrapment is a term that refers to the intentions and actions of law enforcement agents who induce an otherwise unwilling individual to commit a crime for the purposes of criminal prosecution. Any person who is in agreement, collaboration, or cooperation with a law enforcement agent initiating the criminal design may be considered guilty of entrapment. A private citizen who performs the acts of the same nature is not considered guilty of entrapment. A defendant who claims that he/she was entrapped must provide sufficient proof that he/she did not have

Copyright © Mometrix Media. You have been licensed one copy of this document for personal use only. Any other reproduction or redistribution is strictly prohibited. All rights reserved.

predisposition to commit the said crime and that he/she was induced to do so by a law enforcement officer or staff.

Totality of circumstances and bright line standards

The totality of the circumstances standard implies that no single factor, but many factors, facts, and contexts must be considered to make a conclusive decision if there is probable cause, or if a detention is really a detention, or if a person acted under color of law. Precedents are considered to determine if the case meets the criteria. The bright line standard implies the opposite; only one factor is considered to make a decision if there is probable cause. Any unwanted, non-accidental touching of another person comprises a battery. Anybody who has been caught and proved to have performed such acts is accused of battery without consideration for other factors.

Modus operandi

Modus operandi (abbreviated as MO) is a Latin term which means "mode of operation." The phrase is used in investigative terminology and refers to a criminal's characteristic patterns and methods of work. For example, a robber may use a mask or operate only in certain areas, or an Internet thief may use certain hacker programs to get access to data. Some modus operandi may be common for several offenders. Sometimes, however, perpetrators use unique techniques or unusual tools to commit crimes. A criminal's modus operandi may change over time. Police departments keep MO in the profile of each offender and then use it to identify clues to the offender's psychology. Modus operandi should not be confused with a criminal's "signature".

Copyright © Mometrix Media. You have been licensed one copy of this document for personal use only. Any other reproduction or redistribution is strictly prohibited. All rights reserved.

Preparing & Presenting Testimony

Courtroom appearance and conduct

The general rules for appropriate courtroom appearance and conduct during a trial are as follows:

- Familiarize yourself with the courthouse beforehand.
- Keep the case confidential. Do not share any information related to the case in public in order not to be overheard by the opposing side witness, juror, or attorney.
- Keep your private matters confidential. Do not share opinions, biases, and preferences in public for the same reasons.
- Remember to be professional, respectful, courteous, and polite.
- Do not be late on the day of the trial. Allow yourself plenty of time to arrive and settle in.
- Dress appropriately. Formal businesslike attire is considered appropriate for the courtroom appearance.
- Do not contact the defense counsel and witnesses just before the trial in order to avoid provocation.

Preparation for courtroom testimony

Before the testimony, the investigator must make sure that the investigation is complete and the final report is submitted. Then, the investigator should arrange a pre-trial meeting with the attorney who called him/her into court and present the summary of the case along with all materials pertaining to the investigation, such as evidence, photographs, reports, etc. At the meeting the attorney will review the case emphasizing strengths and weaknesses of both sides, and suggest the possible direction of witness questioning for both attorneys. Right before the trial, the investigator should review the case again, focusing on such issues as availability of evidence, legibility of notes, and accurateness of the final report.

Investigator behavior during testimony

The following are the general guidelines for the investigator's behavior during the courtroom testimony.

- The investigator should appear relaxed and behave in a natural manner.
- The investigator should answer only those questions that are addressed to him/her.
- The investigator should refer to his/her final report only when allowed by the court.
- The investigator should describe the crime scene as it was without distortion or exaggeration.
- The investigator should be ready to explain why during the testimony he/she uses details not mentioned in the report.
- The investigator should use clear understandable language and avoid legislative or criminalistics jargon.
- The investigator should speak in a neutral manner avoiding irony and sarcasm.
- The investigator should appear detached.
- The investigator should not explain the law.
- The investigator should take the opportunity to explain him/herself during the rebuttal.

Testimony impeachment

Methods of testimony impeachment are as follows:

- Proving that the witness's previous statements are inconsistent with the courtroom testimony.

Copyright © Mometrix Media. You have been licensed one copy of this document for personal use only. Any other reproduction or redistribution is strictly prohibited. All rights reserved.

- Proving the witness's bias or prejudice based on a relation to the parties involved, personal interest in the outcome of the trial, open hostility towards the opposing party, or other biases.
- Disrupting the witness's credibility by revealing facts about previous convictions or other delinquent characteristics.
- Disrupting the witness's credibility by revealing facts about his/her mental or physical inability to produce accurate observations and recollections.
- Disrupting the witness's credibility by revealing facts about his/her drug or alcohol abuse.
- Showing the erroneousness of the witness's testimony by presenting the facts that prove this erroneousness.

Witness preparation for testimony

It is usually not recommended to rehearse a witness's trial testimony as the witness's answers may appear to be coached. However, the subject matter of the examination should be discussed prior to the examination. The witness's depositions should have been provided to the witness, and any statement that might surface during cross-examination should be discussed. Any interrogatory or other pleading should be discussed with the witness along with any medical record or other document that might be used for cross-examination. If there is evidence that the witness does not want to present because its presentation before the Court and jury might be embarrassing, this evidence should be evaluated. Another effective method to prepare the witness for the trial cross-examination during the deposition is to allow the opposing counsel to attack the witness so that the opposing counsel covers all weak spots at the deposition.

Preparation of different witness types

It is important to tailor witness preparation to meet different types. The profile of the witness is as significant as the facts that witness may respond to. Therefore, the witness's profile must be evaluated prior to depositions and trials. As a result of this evaluation, the investigator must prepare the witness to control his/her own emotions in order to make a good impression on the jury. The following are the most common types of witnesses:

- The "know-it-all" or "that's my story and I'm sticking to it" type – believes that only his/her story is worth listening to
- The "know-nothing" type – knows only a few facts
- The "scared" type – intimidated by litigation process
- The "chatterbox" type – volunteers information
- The minor type – children who feel uncomfortable and intimidated
- The expert type – a witness who possesses professional knowledge of the subject matter.

Know-nothing type
The "know-nothing" type of witness is an individual who possesses knowledge of only one or two facts that are material to any issue in the case. Many of these witnesses may attempt to "contribute more" to the trial by testifying on the facts that they are really not familiar with. Therefore, it is not recommended to suggest to this witness facts that others witnesses or parties might know and that one would have expected this witness to know. The witness should only be asked questions about the facts he/she knows and let go immediately. It is not recommended to lead or direct this witness as his/her credibility may become doubtful.

Know-it-all type
A witness of this type should be made aware of the fact that opposing counsel, the court,

Copyright © Mometrix Media. You have been licensed one copy of this document for personal use only. Any other reproduction or redistribution is strictly prohibited. All rights reserved.

and the jury may not want to know everything that the witness knows and is willing to share. Still, it might be difficult to control the witness, especially during the recollection of a particular set of facts in which the witness believes, regardless of what other evidence might indicate. Often, investigating officers, experts, eye witnesses, and clients who know just a few facts set to impress the opposing counsel, the judge and the jury with their "knowledge," and it may be difficult to dissuade them from their crusade. In these cases, it is safer not to call these "know-it-all" witnesses unless their testimony presents the essence of the claim or is not available from another witness.

Chatterbox type
This type of witness is the most difficult because his/her preparation may demand a lot of character from the counsel. At times, it is necessary to be firm, even insulting. The witness should be familiarized with all the details of the testimony subject matter, and it even might be necessary to coach some questions and answers. Often, the counsel may have to simply object to the volunteered information the witness is so willing to disclose, and advise the witness to only respond to the questions. It may be necessary to interrupt the witness and advise the jury that the question has been answered in full. The witness must be persuaded that the whole purpose is to tell the truth and to impress the jury with the truth.

Scared type
This type of witness may not be able to articulate their true feelings and emotions in front of a jury or opposing counsel. This trait should be identified during the discussion with the client and/or witness prior to deposition or trial. Pre-trial cross-examination is the best method to prepare this witness for deposition or cross-examination. It is necessary to put the witness at ease with the method and subject matter of interrogation. The witness should be convinced that the purpose of interrogation is to seek the truth. This

witness can be dangerous because his/her reaction to the opposing counsel's bullish, arrogant, or condescending behavior may cause the jury to unduly sympathize with such a witness since no juror would like to be put in the same uncomfortable position. These witnesses should be questioned and let go quickly.

Expert type
Before even identifying the expert, the counsel should research his/her background to avoid problems during testimony. In order to prepare the expert witness for deposition or trial testimony, the entire file should be thoroughly examined because the opposing counsel will do the same. Any information in the file that needs explanation should be reviewed with the expert in detail. Any adverse portions of the witness's testimony should be discussed with the witness in order to explain any differences, discrepancies, or inconsistencies. Medical experts should be prepared for testimony in relation to Alabama law. The witness should be cautioned of such peculiarities of Alabama law as the requirements of proof, worsening of a condition as opposed to a loss of a chance, and the proximate causation relative to injury and death.

Minor type
The most important aspect of obtaining testimony from a minor is to make him/her feel comfortable with the counsel and the questions asked. The counsel should spend enough time with the minor to establish rapport and get a candid response. Although leading questions are usually not recommended, the court generally gives great leeway in leading questions addressed to a child. During preparation for testimony, non-leading questions should be used first to observe the witness's reaction and response. Although narrative responses are not favored in court, many courts allow narrative responses from a minor if he/she is responsive to the question. Suggestion should not be used as it may be proved that the parents or guardians made suggestions

Copyright © Mometrix Media. You have been licensed one copy of this document for personal use only. Any other reproduction or redistribution is strictly prohibited. All rights reserved.

during pre-trial discussions. If it appears that the minor's testimony is based on comments which came from a parent or guardian, the credibility of the witness's testimony is compromised.

Deposition testimony witness preparation
Since the deposition testimony usually follows the responses to interrogatories, a good time to start witness preparation is after the interrogatories are answered. The interrogatory answers act as a structure base on which the further discovery will be made. Therefore, the thoroughness and accuracy of the answers should be evaluated. Usually, the questions and answers to interrogatories are provided to parties before the pre-deposition conference. Some of the subjects that should be discussed with the witness are the following:

- Purpose of deposition
- Credibility
- Judgments, guesses, and opinions
- Witness's demeanor and manner of speaking
- Attention to the lawyer's questions
- Giving information voluntarily
- Use of extraneous information, such as notes, documents, diagrams, drawings, etc.
- Right to refuse to answer a question.

Speculation at deposition
Many witnesses hold a firm belief that if they cannot testify the absolute truth, they should not speculate or give opinion. Although there should be no speculation in preparing a witness, the witness should be advised that he/she can give a judgment in response to a question. However, the witness should be cautioned that he/she must be at least familiar with the facts upon which they can give an opinion or judgment. Many witnesses who have heard the term "beyond a reasonable doubt" sometimes feel reluctant to testify about an aspect of the case of which they are not certain. To overcome this reluctance, it is necessary to discuss the issue

of "best judgment" and "opinion" with the witness.

Adverse or incomplete deposition

In case the deposition testimony is adverse, incomplete, or needs further explanation, it is necessary to discuss this portion of the deposition prior to the trial in order to avoid problems at the cross-examination. The witness should be inquired again about the truth of the matter and asked to explain any inconsistencies or gaps in information discovered by the opposing counsel. Often, it is recommended for the witness to admit that the testimony in deposition is wrong and that the witness has made an honest mistake. Juries may forgive honest mistakes or errors but may not be willing to forgive an intentional misrepresentation or an attempt to conceal the truth or be evasive.

Lay witness and expert witness testimonies

Both lay witnesses and expert witnesses may express their opinions during a testimony; the difference is the matters on which they can express their opinions. A lay witness may express his/her opinion on matters which can be commonly observed and which do not require specific professional knowledge, just common sense and logic. The following observations may be supported by a lay witness: color, age, race, sex, weight, height, size, nationality, language, emotional state, speed, intoxication. An expert witness may express opinions on matters which require special education, training, skills, or experience in science, trade, or art. Expert witnesses possess knowledge or practice skills at a level not common among ordinary individuals. Before testifying, expert witnesses must prove their expertise. Examples of matters on which expert witnesses may express opinion include physical and mental health, technical conditions of vehicles, fire arms, equipment, etc.

Copyright © Mometrix Media. You have been licensed one copy of this document for personal use only. Any other reproduction or redistribution is strictly prohibited. All rights reserved.

Hearsay evidence

The term hearsay refers to unverified information, rumors, secondhand statements, etc. Hearsay implies that the information has not been obtained directly by the witness, but was told to the witness by someone else who is not present in court and cannot be questioned. The term hearsay applies to verbal and written statements. Hearsay is generally not admitted in court for the following reasons:

- The person who originally made the statement is not present in court and cannot be put under oath.
- The original author of the statement cannot be cross-examined.
- It is impossible to observe the author's demeanor.
- Errors might occur while information is passed from one person to another.
- In some cases, courts make exceptions to the hearsay rule and consider these statements admissible. The following are some of the exceptions: dying declarations, spontaneous declarations, former testimony, past recollection recorded, business records, confessions and admissions.

Admissible evidence

There are three types of evidence that can be admitted in court:

- Testimony of witnesses – courtroom statements made by individuals who observed, heard, or recalled anything related to any aspect of the crime or incident and are willing to share this knowledge with the court. The witnesses must pass the rule of competence in order to testify in court.
- Documentary evidence – any written, audio, visual, or video documentation related to the investigation, for example, letters, emails, audio

recordings, photographs, video tapes, etc.
- Physical evidence – tangible objects, such as weapons, objects containing fingerprints, bloodstains, fiber, etc. collected during the crime scene processing, or during subsequent stages of the investigation.

Spontaneous declaration

Spontaneous declaration, or res gestae, is an exclamation or an utterance made in response to some shocking event, such as a crime. For the spontaneous declaration to be admissible in court, it must be proved that the shocking event actually took place, and that the statement was natural and involuntary. The witness who was present at the time the spontaneous declaration was made can testify and present the statement as evidence. One of the reasons why spontaneous declarations are admitted in court is the unusual circumstances under which the statement was made. These circumstances make the statement trustworthy and therefore can be used as evidence. An example of a spontaneous declaration would be an exclamation "He has a knife!" or "He just shot him!"

Dying declaration

The dying declaration is a statement made by an individual under a sense of impending death that explains the cause of death. The dying declaration of a victim who identified the suspect or made a statement about circumstances of the death is admissible in court. For the dying declaration to be admitted in court, it must be proved that the individual was dying while making the statement, died after making the statement, and was mentally capable while making the statement. One of the reasons why a dying declaration is admissible in court is the fact that in many cases the killer and the victim were the only persons present at the crime scene and there are no other witnesses.

Copyright © Mometrix Media. You have been licensed one copy of this document for personal use only. Any other reproduction or redistribution is strictly prohibited. All rights reserved.

Another reason why dying declarations are admitted in court is because the circumstances of the statement make it trustworthy.

Past recollection recorded

Past recollection recorded is a term that refers to a memorandum or any other record documenting a matter about which a witness once had knowledge but now his/her recollection is insufficient to allow the witness to make a complete and accurate testimony. It must be proved that the recollection recorded has been made or adopted by the witness when the matter was still fresh in the witness's memory and that the recollection is a correct reflection of the prior knowledge. The memorandum or record is read into evidence but may not itself be admitted as evidence unless an adverse party agreed to it. An example of a past recollection recorded may be the investigator's notes.

Former testimony

The former testimony refers to the testimony made prior to the present proceeding at another hearing of the same or a different proceeding by a witness who is currently unavailable for questioning. The testimony must be given as a witness or in a deposition taken in compliance with law during the same or different proceeding. The subject against whom the testimony is used must have had an opportunity and similar motive to develop the testimony by direct, cross, or redirect examination. The former testimony can be considered admissible only when it is proved that the witness is not available for cross-examination. The main reasons why the former testimony is admitted in court is the unavailability of the witness and the proved lawfulness of his/her prior statement.

Admissibility of confessions and admissions

Confessions and admissions, which are acknowledgements of guilt, are considered admissible in court on the presumption that a person would not be likely to confess to a crime or admit the wrongdoing unless he/she committed this crime or was involved in the wrongdoing. The evidence of confession or admission can be admitted through an investigator who obtained the said confession or admission. Usually confessions are documented either in the form of a written statement or videotaped. However, if the suspect's confession was unexpected, the investigator may have had to rely on his/her note taking skills to record the confession. In this case, the investigator should refer to his/her notes while making a court testimony.

Business records

Business records are any form of memoranda, reports, records, or data compilations documenting acts, events, conditions, opinions, or diagnoses, made by a person with knowledge of the conducted business activity. For a business record to be admissible in court, it must be proven that it was the regular practice of that business activity to make the memorandum, report, record, or data compilation, as shown by the testimony of the custodian or other qualified witness. Trustworthiness of the method or circumstances of preparation must also be proven. The term "business" used in this explanation refers to business, institution, association, profession, occupation, and calling of every kind, conducted for profit or not. An example of business record would be a registry of guests checking in and out of a hotel.

Judicial notice

Judicial notice is a term that refers to the concept based on the presumption that the court does not require presentation of certain

Copyright © Mometrix Media. You have been licensed one copy of this document for personal use only. Any other reproduction or redistribution is strictly prohibited. All rights reserved.

types of evidence to prove certain facts because the court is authorized to verify these facts without proof. A judicially noticed fact must not be subject to reasonable dispute; it must be generally known within the territorial jurisdiction of the trial court, or the court must be capable of verifying the fact by resorting to sources whose accuracy cannot reasonably be questioned. A court does not need a request to take judicial notice, but is obliged to do so if requested by a party and supplied with the necessary information. Judicial notice may be taken at any stage of the legal proceeding.

Admissibility of character evidence

Rule 404 of the Federal Rules of Evidence proclaims that "evidence of a person's character or a trait of character is not admissible for the purpose of proving action in conformity therewith on a particular occasion". However, there are the following exceptions to this rule:
- Evidence of a trait of character of the accused is pertinent to the crime committed.
- Evidence of a trait of character of the alleged victim of the crime is offered by an accused and admitted under Rule 404(a)(2).
- Evidence of the same trait of character of the accused offered by the prosecution.
- Evidence of a character trait of peacefulness of the alleged victim is offered by the prosecution in a homicide case in response to the evidence that the alleged victim was the first aggressor.
- Evidence of the truthful or untruthful character of a witness as provided in Rule 608.

Presumption of innocence

Presumption of innocence is a term that refers to the legal right which states that no person shall be considered guilty until convicted by a court. The prosecution bears the burden of proof, which means that the prosecution attorney has to convince the court of the accused person's guilt beyond a reasonable doubt. The defense attorney does not have to prove the accused person's innocence but he/she has to produce evidence that would show that there is a doubt in the guilt of the accused. Presumption of innocence is usually enjoyed by the accused in criminal trials. In civil actions and proceedings not covered by Act of Congress or by Federal Rules of Evidence, a presumption of innocence implies that the party against whom it is directed bears the burden of producing evidence to rebut or meet the presumption.

Sixth Amendment

The Sixth Amendment protects the defendant from biases and prejudices. It guarantees that "in all criminal prosecutions, the accused shall enjoy the right to a speedy and public trial, by an impartial jury of the State and district wherein the crime shall have been committed, which district shall have been previously ascertained by law, and to be informed of the nature and cause of the accusation; to be confronted with the witnesses against him; to have compulsory process for obtaining witnesses in his favor, and to have the Assistance of Counsel for his defense". The Amendment ensures that the defendant receives proper counseling during all stages of the criminal justice process, from pre-trial custody to appellation of the sentence.

Eighth Amendment

The Eighth Amendment which guarantees that "excessive bail shall not be required," ensures that all defendants have fair rights to be bailed out for the time between the arrest and the trial. If the defendant fails to appear at the trial, he/she has to bear the cost of the bail. The Eighth Amendment does not guarantee bail to all defendants; however, it requires that bail should not be excessive.

Copyright © Mometrix Media. You have been licensed one copy of this document for personal use only. Any other reproduction or redistribution is strictly prohibited. All rights reserved.

The text of the Amendment proclaims that excessive fines shall not be imposed, "nor cruel and unusual punishments inflicted". This text is used to protect inmates of correctional facilities from unfair treatment from guards as well as in cases of death penalty sentences.

Fourteenth Amendment

Section 1 of the Fourteenth Amendment proclaims that "All persons born or naturalized in the United States and subject to the jurisdiction thereof, are citizens of the United States and of the State wherein they reside. No State shall make or enforce any law which shall abridge the privileges or immunities of citizens of the United States; nor shall any State deprive any person of life, liberty, or property, without due process of law; nor deny to any person within its jurisdiction the equal protection of the laws." This section is used to protect defendants from state criminal prosecution by assuming that suspects accused of state crimes have the same rights as suspects accused of federal crimes.

Copyright © Mometrix Media. You have been licensed one copy of this document for personal use only. Any other reproduction or redistribution is strictly prohibited. All rights reserved.

Practice Test

Practice Questions

1. Which of the following types of records are NOT made available to the public by the Freedom of Information Act?
    a. FBI records
    b. Records held by the United States Congress
    c. Social Security Administration records
    d. Military records

2. When a private investigator is the first to arrive at a crime scene, what should his or her initial action be?
    a. Calling the police
    b. Dusting for prints
    c. Photographing the scene
    d. Sealing the exits

3. Which of the following forms of hearsay would most likely be admissible in court?
    a. A statement describing plans to commit a crime in the future.
    b. A statement made in the heat of passion.
    c. A statement made by a witness on his or her deathbed.
    d. All of the above

4. Which of the following is a potential problem with the "pride and ego down" interrogation technique?
    a. It is extremely time-consuming.
    b. It often results in physical violence.
    c. It risks forming too strong of a bond between the interrogator and the subject.
    d. If it fails, it may be difficult for the interrogation to continue.

5. For which assignment would a ghillie suit be most appropriate?
    a. Indoor surveillance
    b. Outdoor surveillance
    c. Surveillance on foot
    d. Moving surveillance

6. Which of the following would be the best question during an interrogation?
    a. "You were at the bowling alley last night, weren't you?
    b. "Were you at the bowling alley last light?"
    c. "Why were you at the bowling alley last night?"
    d. "You weren't at the bowling alley last night, were you?"

Copyright © Mometrix Media. You have been licensed one copy of this document for personal use only. Any other reproduction or redistribution is strictly prohibited. All rights reserved.

7. Which of the following statements about circumstantial evidence is true?

    a. If there is enough of it, it can be sufficient to build a case.
    b. It directly proves the existence of a fact.
    c. It does not point towards a specific conclusion.
    d. It is considered stronger than direct evidence.

8. Which tool of crime scene documentation is used to describe the collection of evidence?
    a. Latent print lift log
    b. Scene description worksheet
    c. General worksheet
    d. Photographic log

9. Which of the following is an example of circumstantial evidence?
    a. The defendant owned the same type of weapon that was used to injure the victim of an assault.
    b. The defendant's fingerprints were found on the murder weapon.
    c. A witness claims to have heard the victim shout the defendant's name during the attack.
    d. The government produces official records indicating that the defendant committed tax fraud.

10. Which party bears the burden of proof in a criminal trial?
    a. Government
    b. Private investigator
    c. Defense
    d. Prosecution

11. Which of the following is a focus of criminalistics?
    a. Toxicology
    b. Odontology
    c. Pathology
    d. Voice spectroscopy

12. Which piece of legislation requires agencies to notify the public when the agency maintains records that can be searched by name?
    a. Fair Credit Reporting Act of 1970
    b. Freedom of Information Act of 1966
    c. Privacy Act of 1974
    d. E-Government Act of 2002

13. Which of the following is a disadvantage for a private investigator of having an attorney as a client?
    a. The private investigator's notes are available to the opposing side during trial.
    b. Attorneys are often reluctant to make advance payments.
    c. The private investigator must lobby to have his or her work classified as attorney work product.
    d. Working for attorneys tends to be less lucrative for private investigators.

Copyright © Mometrix Media. You have been licensed one copy of this document for personal use only. Any other reproduction or redistribution is strictly prohibited. All rights reserved.

14. When following a vehicle on a multi-lane road, where is the ideal place for a private investigator to position him or herself?

    a. In a lane to the right, approximately one car length behind
    b. In a lane to the left, approximately three car lengths behind
    c. In the same lane, two car lengths behind
    d. In the same lane, ten car lengths behind

15. If "don*" is entered into a search engine, which of the following results would NOT appear?
    a. Donald
    b. Don
    c. Donor
    d. Donkey

16. Which of the following is NOT one of the criteria of competence for a witness in court?
    a. The witness must have personal experience related to his or her testimony.
    b. The witness must be able to communicate what he or she has experienced.
    c. The witness' testimony must relate to the case.
    d. The witness must take the oath and be capable of understanding it.

17. The federal government's PACER service provides access to...
    a. Criminal records.
    b. Medical records.
    c. Court records.
    d. Academic records.

18. What is the most prevalent criticism of the Reid technique?
    a. It produces false confessions.
    b. It violates basic human rights.
    c. It requires too much training.
    d. It is too expensive.

19. Which of the following subjects may an investigator inquire about during a pre-employment screening interview?
    a. Religion
    b. Disability
    c. Sexual orientation
    d. Driving record

20. Which of the following statements about process service is true in most states?
    a. The documents must be in a sealed envelope.
    b. Process may be served to any employee of a target corporation.
    c. Service of process does not have to be in person.
    d. The documents may be served even if the recipient refuses to accept them.

Copyright © Mometrix Media. You have been licensed one copy of this document for personal use only. Any other reproduction or redistribution is strictly prohibited. All rights reserved.

21. When are most civil trials settled?
    a. Before discovery
    b. After discovery
    c. During discovery
    d. None of the above

22. Which of the following communications are illegal to intercept under Title III?
    a. Electronic
    b. Oral
    c. Wire
    d. All of the above

23. Which of the following records are NOT subject to regulation by the Fair Credit Reporting Act of 1970?
    a. Employment history
    b. Insurance claims
    c. Academic records
    d. Medical records

24. In which of the following cases would a citizen's arrest be permissible?
    a. The citizen suspects that a misdemeanor has been committed.
    b. The arrest would prevent a theft.
    c. The citizen is a former law enforcement officer.
    d. All of the above

25. What type of evidence is a DNA sample?
    a. Real evidence
    b. Demonstrative evidence
    c. Documentary evidence
    d. Testimonial evidence

26. Which of the following statements about partial fingerprints is true?
    a. Partial fingerprints are admissible as evidence in court.
    b. Partial fingerprints are found less often than full fingerprints.
    c. Partial fingerprints are easier to lift than full fingerprints.
    d. Partial fingerprints are rarely smudged.

27. A private investigator records a telephone conversation between his client in the United States and a business associate in Canada. The client resides in a state with one-party consent laws. The business associate is not aware that the call is being recorded. Will this recording be admissible in court?
    a. Yes, because international calls are not subject to recording restrictions based on consent.
    b. Yes, because Canada also allows one-party consent.
    c. No, because international calls always require all-party consent.
    d. No, because Canada forbids the recording of any telephone calls.

Copyright © Mometrix Media. You have been licensed one copy of this document for personal use only. Any other reproduction or redistribution is strictly prohibited. All rights reserved.

28. Under what circumstances may business records be admitted in court as hearsay evidence?
    a. The records establish facts contrary to the case being made by one party to the trial.
    b. The records are introduced and placed into context by a qualified witness.
    c. The records were made around the same time as the trial.
    d. The records have been maintained properly.

29. Which field test is used to determine whether blood found at a crime scene is from a human being?
    a. Kastle-Meyer
    b. Leuchomalachite green
    c. Luminol
    d. Precipitin

30. Which of the following is an example of permissible deception for a private investigator?
    a. Telling a suspect that he must confess or else his son will be injured
    b. Impersonating a police officer
    c. Impersonating a doctor
    d. Telling a suspect that his girlfriend has implicated him in a crime

31. Which of the following is NOT an element of fraud?
    a. Misrepresentation of a material fact
    b. Damages caused by the misrepresentation
    c. Inability of the victim to identify the misrepresentation
    d. Intention to misrepresent and defraud

32. Identify one difference between arrest and detention.
    a. Arrest requires probable cause that a crime has been committed.
    b. Arrest requires reasonable suspicion that a crime has been committed.
    c. Detention may not include a pat-down for weapons.
    d. Detention may not last more than five minutes.

33. Under what circumstances should a private investigator return the original signed copy of a statement to the interviewee?
    a. When the interviewee requests the original signed copy of the statement.
    b. When the interviewee offers to pay for the original signed copy of the statement.
    c. When the interviewee wants to retract the statement.
    d. A private investigator should never return the original signed copy of a statement to the interviewee.

34. Which of the following actions may a bounty hunter perform that a law enforcement officer may not?
    a. A bounty hunter may read a suspect his or her rights.
    b. A bounty hunter may arrest a suspect at any time.
    c. A bounty hunter may search a suspect's house without a warrant.
    d. A bounty hunter may enter any residence.

Copyright © Mometrix Media. You have been licensed one copy of this document for personal use only. Any other reproduction or redistribution is strictly prohibited. All rights reserved.

35. Which of the following reasons explains why an offender might claim to have witnessed a crime he or she committed?
    a. The offender hopes to find out what information the police already have.
    b. The offender wants to provide false information to confuse the police.
    c. The offender hopes to deflect attention from him or herself.
    d. All of the above

36. What level of evidence is required in a civil court?
    a. Preponderance of evidence
    b. Evidence beyond a reasonable doubt
    c. Clear and convincing evidence
    d. None of the above

37. Which of the following is an example of demonstrative evidence?
    a. Murder weapon
    b. Computer simulation
    c. E-mail
    d. Deposition

38. Which of the following devices can interfere with wireless cameras?
    a. Blender
    b. Microwave ovens
    c. Land line telephone
    d. Radio

39. Which tool of crime scene documentation is used to create a narrative of the event?
    a. Latent print lift log
    b. General worksheet
    c. Scene description worksheet
    d. Evidence log

40. Which piece of legislation entitles citizens to one free credit report every year?
    a. Fair and Accurate Credit Transactions Act of 2003
    b. Fair Credit Reporting Act of 1970
    c. Fair Credit Billing Act of 1975
    d. Truth in Lending Act of 1968

41. Which type of missing person is typically the most difficult to find?
    a. Tenant skip
    b. Missing heir
    c. Unclaimed property owner
    d. Birth parent of an adopted child

42. Which of the following is NOT one of the three types of relationship abuse identified by the Centers for Disease Control?
    a. Physical abuse
    b. Emotional abuse
    c. Sexual abuse
    d. Chronic abuse

Copyright © Mometrix Media. You have been licensed one copy of this document for personal use only. Any other reproduction or redistribution is strictly prohibited. All rights reserved.

43. An oral statement made outside of the courtroom and then introduced during trial is called a(n)...
    a. Interrogatory.
    b. Deposition.
    c. Initial conference.
    d. Request for production.

44. In which of the following places is it most likely legal to install hidden cameras?
    a. Private room
    b. Public bathroom
    c. Hotel room
    d. Dormitory hall

45. Which of the following statements about recording cell phone conversations is true?
    a. Neither party to the conversation needs to consent.
    b. One party to the conversation needs to consent.
    c. Both parties to the conversation need to consent.
    d. A magistrate must consent.

46. Which types of businesses are subject to the Fair Credit Reporting Act?
    a. Database companies
    b. Consumer credit reporting companies
    c. Both A and B
    d. Neither A nor B

47. The National Association of Legal Investigators has modeled its code of ethics after the code of the...
    a. American Bar Association.
    b. United States Association of Professional Investigators.
    c. National Association of Investigative Specialists.
    d. World Association of Private Investigators.

48. What device is used to record the numbers dialed for outgoing calls on a telephone?
    a. Bug
    b. Pen register
    c. Trap and trace device
    d. Wire

49. In which of the following scenarios may an attorney reveal information about a client?
    a. When doing so would help establish a defense for the attorney against criminal prosecution
    b. When doing so would prevent substantial bodily harm to the client
    c. Both A and B
    d. Neither A nor B

50. In which direction do subjects typically look when they are recalling information?
    a. Up
    b. Down
    c. Left
    d. Right

Copyright © Mometrix Media. You have been licensed one copy of this document for personal use only. Any other reproduction or redistribution is strictly prohibited. All rights reserved.

Answers and Explanations

1. B: Records held by the United States Congress are not made available to the public by the Freedom of Information Act (FOIA). However, FBI records, military and defense records, Social Security Administration records, and Veteran's Administration records are all available to the public through FOIA requests. The Freedom of Information Act was passed in 1966 so that public records could be accessible. The act declares that citizens have a right to this information, whereas in the past the public's access was limited to those documents containing information which a citizen might "need to know."

2. A: When a private investigator is the first person to arrive at a crime scene, his or her initial action should be to call the police. The only exception to this rule is if there is an injured or endangered person, in which case the private investigator should provide assistance. Most of the time, a private investigator will not have access to a crime scene until after the police have finished their work. Before entering a crime scene, the investigator should always check with the police. It is all too easy to contaminate a crime scene inadvertently.

3. D: All of the above statements would most likely be admissible in court. Hearsay evidence is the introduction or reporting of a statement made by someone other than the witness who is currently testifying. In most situations, hearsay evidence is inadmissible in court. However, a judge will often allow hearsay evidence if it entails plans to commit a crime in the future, or if it is made in the heat of passion. With regard to the latter scenario, the courts recognize that people often make incriminating or telling remarks in a moment of excitement and then either do not remember making the statement or deny having made it. In general, the courts will allow these remarks to be introduced as evidence. In similar fashion, the courts will often admit statements made by a witness on his or her deathbed as evidence. Not only would it be impossible for the witness to appear in court, but it may be presumed that a dying person has less incentive to lie.

4. D: One potential problem with the "pride and ego down" interrogation technique is that, if it fails, it may be difficult for the interrogation to continue. This interrogation technique was developed by the United States military. In brief, it entails criticizing the subject so that he or she feels compelled to respond and, in doing so, possibly revealing more information than he or she should. There is the risk, however, that the subject will simply be offended or will refuse to cooperate, and the interrogation will be difficult to continue.

5. B: A ghillie suit would be most appropriate for outdoor surveillance. Ghillie suits are special costumes that appear to be made of sticks and leaves. They are designed to provide camouflage in a forest setting. Of course, it is necessary for such a suit to match the color and type of foliage that is prevalent at the time. It should be noted that a ghillie suit is best for situations in which the investigator will not have to move for a long time. In other words, a ghillie suit is a good option for long stake-outs, but not for tailing a suspect.

6. C: Of the given questions, the best for an interrogation would be "Why were you at the bowling alley last night?" The interrogator should avoid asking leading questions: that is,

Copyright © Mometrix Media. You have been licensed one copy of this document for personal use only. Any other reproduction or redistribution is strictly prohibited. All rights reserved.

questions that suggest an answer. Answer choice A encourages the interviewee to answer "Yes," and answer choice D encourages the interviewee to answer "No." An interrogator should also avoid asking questions that elicit only a one-word answer. It is better to ask an open-ended question so that the interviewee will feel compelled to add some detail. The best interrogation questions are those that lead to more lines of inquiry.

7. A: If there is enough circumstantial evidence, it can be sufficient to build a case. Circumstantial evidence does not directly prove anything, but it suggests a conclusion. For instance, if a suspect is seen in the area in which a crime is committed, and the suspect is known to possess the weapon with which the crime was committed, these facts would be admissible as circumstantial evidence. If the prosecution is able to gather enough circumstantial evidence, it may be possible to support a case on this basis. Circumstantial evidence is not considered stronger than direct evidence.

8. C: A general worksheet is used to describe the collection of evidence. The general worksheet is one of the six primary documents required at a crime scene; the others are the scene description worksheet, the diagram log, the photographic log, the latent print log, and the evidence log. The latent print log is used to store and record the source of latent fingerprints. The scene description worksheet provides a basic summary of the crime event, as well as any pertinent observations about the crime scene. The photographic log is a set of pictures of the scene.

9. A: If the defendant owned the same type of weapon that was used to injure the victim, this would be an example of circumstantial evidence. Circumstantial evidence suggests a conclusion, but does not prove anything directly. In order to form the basis of a case, circumstantial evidence must be either overwhelming or accompanied by direct evidence or testimony. Fingerprints on a murder weapon would be considered direct evidence. Official government records or a witness' recollection of a victim's cry would both be considered hearsay, though both of these would most likely be admissible in court.

10. D: In a criminal trial, the prosecution bears the burden of proof. The burden of proof is the responsibility for proving the case. In the United States criminal court system, the burden of proof lies with the prosecution, meaning that the defendant is innocent until proven guilty. The prosecution must prove guilt beyond a reasonable doubt in order for the defendant to be found guilty.

11. D: Voice spectroscopy is a focus of criminalistics. Criminalistics is the use of scientific techniques for gathering and evaluating physical evidence. Voice spectroscopy is analysis of the wave characteristics of a voice sample. Some of the other disciplines in criminalistics are chemistry, photography, fingerprinting, lie detection, and document authorization. Toxicology, odontology, and pathology are all elements of forensic medicine, which is the other main branch of forensics. Forensic medicine is the application of medical techniques to criminal cases. Toxicology is the analysis of drugs and poisons. Odontology is the analysis of dental records and artifacts. Pathology is the study of diseases.

12. C: The Privacy Act of 1974 requires agencies to notify the public when the agency maintains records that can be searched by name. If a personal record could be obtained from the agency by giving the name of the record holder, the existence of this record must be declared by the agency. The Privacy Act is in some ways the obverse of the Freedom of Information Act of 1966, which grants the public the right to access files at its own

Copyright © Mometrix Media. You have been licensed one copy of this document for personal use only. Any other reproduction or redistribution is strictly prohibited. All rights reserved.

discretion. The Fair Credit Reporting Act of 1970 regulates the collection and distribution of consumer information. The E-Government Act of 2002 established a bureaucratic framework for providing the public with electronic access to government records.

13. B: One disadvantage for a private investigator of having an attorney as a client is that attorneys are often reluctant to make advance payments. Attorneys are apt to wait to make payment until the private investigator has finished his or her work. This can be inconvenient for the investigator. On the other hand, any notes made by the private investigator will not be available to the other side during the discovery phase of a trial. This is because the work of the private investigator is defined automatically as attorney work product, which is the set of privileged documents an attorney uses to formulate his or her strategy. These documents are protected from discovery by Exemption 5 of the Freedom of Information Act. Finally, most private investigators find working with attorneys to be quite lucrative.

14. A: When following a vehicle on a multi-lane road, the ideal place for a private investigator to position him or herself is in a lane to the right, approximately one car length behind. This places the investigator's vehicle in the target's blind spot. Unless it is necessary, the investigator should try to avoid being directly behind the suspect. Under no circumstances should the investigator drive ahead of the target. An investigator should try to drive an uninteresting and inconspicuous car, neither extremely old nor extremely new. Flashy colors should be avoided as well.

15. B: If "don*" is entered into a search engine, then "Don" would not appear among the search results. Placing an asterisk in a search term is known as using a wild card. It asks the search engine to find any words beginning with the given letters, no matter what the remaining letters may be. Wild cards can be placed at the beginning or the end of a word. They are useful when only part of the word is known.

16. C: The relevance of a witness' testimony is not one of the criteria of competence for a witness in court. Indeed, along with competence and materiality, relevance is one of the three necessary conditions for testimony to be admissible in court. Evidence is considered material if it has clear and direct bearing on the case. The relevance of evidence is its logical connection to the case. The competence of evidence, or a witness, is the extent to which it can be relied upon as accurate and reliable. There are four criteria of competence for a witness: the ability to take and understand the oath, personal knowledge about the testimony to be given, an ability to remember what he or she has experienced, and the ability to communicate this experience.

17. C: The federal government's PACER service provides access to court records. PACER (Public Access to Court Electronic Records) allows citizens to acquire case and docket information from appellate, district, and bankruptcy courts. Private investigators find this to be an invaluable resource for information about legal proceedings.

18. A: The most prevalent criticism of the Reid technique is that it produces false confessions. The Reid technique is a system of interrogation in which the investigator attempts to coax the suspect into confessing. The technique begins with a direct confrontation, in which the investigator indicates that there is significant evidence of guilt on the part of the suspect. The morally dubious part of the technique is its reliance on suggestion and justification, meaning that the investigator attempts to persuade the suspect

- 104 -

Copyright © Mometrix Media. You have been licensed one copy of this document for personal use only. Any other reproduction or redistribution is strictly prohibited. All rights reserved.

that committing the crime was not really such a bad thing. This technique is also known to encourage false confessions.

19. D: An investigator may inquire about a potential employee's driving record during a pre-employment screening interview. Similarly, investigators are allowed to inquire about academic records, credit history, personal references, and criminal records. However, privacy laws prevent investigators from inquiring about a potential employee's religion, disability, or sexual orientation. In addition, investigators are not allowed to ask about ethnicity, marital status, or political affiliation.

20. D: In most states, process documents may still be served if the recipient refuses to accept them. This is known as drop service. In the United States, process documents must be visible to the recipient, and therefore cannot be in a sealed envelope. Documents may only be served to a registered agent of a target corporation. Finally, it is necessary for service of process to be in person.

21. B: Most civil trials are settled after discovery. In the American legal system, discovery is the period during which each side may obtain information from the other. The discovery process typically indicates to both parties the relative strength of each side, so the party with the admittedly weaker case is often ready to make a deal before the trial begins.

22. D: Title III makes it illegal to intercept electronic, oral, and wire communications. Title III is the common title for the Federal Wiretap Act of 1968. This federal law does permit business owners to monitor employee conversations while employees are at work. The business owner is not allowed to record personal conversations conducted over an office phone during the work day, but may use any discussion of criminal activity as evidence in court.

23. C: The Fair Credit Reporting Act of 1970 does not regulate academic records. Medical records, residential history, check writing history, employment history, and insurance claims are all subject to regulation by the FCRA. Any agency that handles these records is designated as a consumer reporting agency, which means the agency must notify consumers about their records, in particular those that include negative information.

24. B: A citizen's arrest would be permissible if it would prevent a theft. Citizen's arrests are rarely necessary or advisable, but a private investigator should nevertheless be aware of the situations in which such an arrest is legal. A private citizen may make an arrest if he or she has witnessed the commission of a felony or breach of the peace. Some states permit citizens to make arrests with only the reasonable suspicion of a felony or breach of the peace. A citizen may also make an arrest if he or she has a warrant on which he or she is identified as the appointed arrester. A citizen's arrest is legal if it is performed while assisting a law enforcement officer. A citizen is not entitled to make arrests simply because he or she is a former law enforcement officer.

25. A: A DNA sample is real evidence. Real evidence is physical material that is directly involved in a case. Real evidence could include things like bloody clothing, weapons, or hair samples. The other three types of evidence are demonstrative, documentary, and testimonial. Demonstrative evidence is an image or representation of something related to the case. For example, real evidence might include maps, audio recordings, or models. Documentary evidence is any records that pertain to the case. Documentary evidence could

Copyright © Mometrix Media. You have been licensed one copy of this document for personal use only. Any other reproduction or redistribution is strictly prohibited. All rights reserved.

include wills, contracts, letters, and emails. If a document is presented because it contains evidence (e.g., fingerprints), it is classified as real evidence. Finally, testimonial evidence is the statements, either spoken or written, of people involved in the case.

26. A: Partial fingerprints are admissible as evidence in court. This is fortunate because partial prints are found much more often than full prints. Finding and lifting partial prints is extremely difficult, however, so private investigators are advised to receive professional assistance unless they have been comprehensively trained in the subject. Partial fingerprints are often smudged, which can render them useless.

27. B: This recording will be admissible in court, because Canada also allows one-party consent. The same is true of the United Kingdom. When one of the countries or states involved in a call has all-party consent laws, it should be assumed that the courts will apply the stricter set of laws. In other words, when a person in a state with one-party consent calls a person in a state with all-party consent, an investigator should have the consent of all parties before recording the conversation.

28. B: Business records may be admitted in court as hearsay evidence when the records are introduced and placed into context by a qualified witness. The witness must be able to identify the records and explain how they were produced. Some hearsay testimony may be admitted if it runs counter to a party's interest, but business records are not an example of this testimony. Official government records may be admitted as hearsay evidence so long as they are properly maintained, but normal business records are subject to a higher standard. The time at which the records were created does not bear on their admissibility.

29. D: A precipitin test is used to determine whether the blood found at a crime scene is from a human being. This test assesses the proteins in the sample, which indicate the species. The other answer choices are presumptive blood tests, meaning that they detect the presence of blood without providing any information about its origin. The Kastle-Meyer test, also known as the phenolphthalein test, begins with the collection of a sample. Ethanol and phenolphthalein are then added to the sample, and if no blood is indicated, peroxide may be added as well. If blood is present, the sample will turn pink. The leuchomalachite green test is much like the Kastle-Meyer test, except leuchomalachite green is used instead of phenolphthalein. The presence of blood in a leuchomalachite green test is indicated by the appearance of a greenish tint. In the luminol test, the presence of blood will be indicated by the appearance of a blue-green glow. One problem with this test is that saliva and bleach may produce a similar glow.

30. D: Telling a suspect that his girlfriend has implicated him in a crime is an example of permissible deception. In general, law enforcement officers and private investigators are allowed to lie when it will not harm or endanger an innocent person or encourage an innocent person to make a false confession. Telling a suspect that he must confess or else his son will be injured exceeds the bounds of morality and legality. Many people would confess to a crime they did not commit under these circumstances. Similarly, impersonating a police officer or doctor is not allowed, because people in these positions elicit a higher level of trust from citizens.

31. C: The inability of the victim to identify the misrepresentation is not an element of fraud. There are some situations in which the victim could be reasonably expected to identify a misrepresentation, but the fraudster will usually be held accountable for the intentional

Copyright © Mometrix Media. You have been licensed one copy of this document for personal use only. Any other reproduction or redistribution is strictly prohibited. All rights reserved.

misrepresentation of fact. The basic elements of fraud are the misrepresentation of a material fact, the intention to misrepresent and defraud, action by the defrauded party based on the misrepresentation, and damages caused by the misrepresentation.

32. A: One difference between arrest and detention is that an arrest requires probable cause that a crime has been committed. Probable cause is a higher burden of proof than reasonable suspicion, which is all that is required for a detention. A detention may include a pat-down for weapons, so long as there is a reasonable suspicion that the detained person is armed. Finally, it has generally been established that a suspect may be detained for as long as 20 minutes without being arrested or having his or her rights violated.

33. D: A private investigator should never return the original signed copy of a statement to the interviewee. Once the statement has been completed, the interviewee should sign it and place his or her initials on each page. The investigator should then put the copy away where the interviewee cannot see it. Many times, an interviewee will become nervous about his or her statement, and will ask to take it back. The investigator should keep a copy of the statement for the interviewee, but should never hand back the original. Returning the original risks seeing it damaged or destroyed, which can be devastating to a case.

34. C: Unlike a law enforcement officer, a bounty hunter may search a suspect's house without a warrant. Bounty hunters typically work in cooperation with a bail bonds office. When a person tries to run away without paying his or her bond, a bounty hunter will be hired to find the bail jumper. Bounty hunters, also known as bail enforcement agents, are not required to read suspects their rights, although law enforcement officials are. Bounty hunters may not arrest a suspect except during the period specified in the hunter's contract. Bounty hunters may not enter any residence besides the residence of the suspect.

35. D: Any of the given reasons might explain why an offender would claim to have witnessed a crime he or she committed. This phenomenon is much more common than most people would expect. Many criminal offenders are paranoid and feel compelled to involve themselves in the investigation so that they can learn how much information the police already have. The offender may also want to confuse the police, or to direct the investigation away from him or herself. A criminal offender may also be enamored with the idea that he or she is at the center of an exciting event, and may simply want to enjoy proximity to the situation.

36. A: In a civil court, a preponderance of evidence is required for a conviction. This is the least amount of evidence required in any court. A preponderance of evidence simply suggests that the defendant is more likely to be guilty than not guilty. In a criminal court, the standard for evidence is that it must prove guilt beyond a reasonable doubt. This does not mean that guilt must be proven absolutely, only that a reasonable person would find no cause for significant doubt. Cases that come before the House Judiciary Committee require clear and convincing evidence. This is considered to be a lower standard than beyond a reasonable doubt. In order for evidence to be defined as clear and convincing, it must obviously support one side more than the other.

37. B: A computer simulation is an example of demonstrative evidence. Demonstrative evidence is any image or representation of a crime scene, a crime, or an object relevant to a crime. Other examples of demonstrative evidence are illustrations, maps, video recordings, and photographs. A murder weapon is classified as real evidence because it is an object

Copyright © Mometrix Media. You have been licensed one copy of this document for personal use only. Any other reproduction or redistribution is strictly prohibited. All rights reserved.

directly involved in the commission of a crime. E-mails are classified as documentary evidence because the content rather than the physical characteristics are important. Depositions, interviews and confessions are considered testimonial evidence.

38. B: Microwave ovens can interfere with wireless cameras, as can portable phones and other electronic items. For this reason, a private investigator should be wary about placing wireless cameras in areas where they could be vulnerable to interference. Also, wireless cameras have a limited transmission range, so they cannot be relied upon to provide images over a long distance. Wireless cameras are more elegant and less obtrusive, but they must be used properly in order to be effective.

39. C: A scene description worksheet is used to create a narrative of an event. This is a general form on which the investigator will record any pertinent information about the scene, as well as a basic description of what is believed to have happened there. The description should include details like the lighting, the furniture, and the signs of struggle or theft. A latent print lift log is used to collect and store fingerprints, as well as to document where they were obtained. A general worksheet is a record of all the evidence found at the crime scene, including where and how it was obtained. The general worksheet may also include some information about possible suspects. Finally, the evidence log is a record of how evidence was collected and marked.

40. A: The Fair and Accurate Credit Transactions Act of 2003 entitles citizens to one free credit report every year. This act was an amendment to the Fair Credit Reporting Act of 1970, which established the consumer reporting agencies that are responsible for issuing these credit reports. The Fair Credit Billing Act of 1975 outlawed unethical practices related to credit card billing. The Truth in Lending Act of 1968 established standards for how borrowing costs are communicated and created.

41. A: Of the given types of missing person, a tenant skip is typically the most difficult to identify. A tenant skip is a person who has disappeared to avoid paying his or her rent. A tenant skip may be escaping the rent associated with a commercial or residential property. A tenant skip is more difficult to find than a missing heir, an unclaimed property owner, or the birth parent of an adopted child because he or she is purposefully hiding. The birth parent of an adopted child may not wish to be found, but it is unlikely that this person will have taken extreme steps to hide his or her identity. Missing heirs and unclaimed property owners are typically not missing on purpose, and are therefore much easier to find.

42. D: Chronic abuse is not one of the three types of relationship abuse identified by the Centers for Disease Control. Instead, the CDC declares that relationship abuse is physical, emotional, or sexual. Physical abuse is violent contact. Emotional abuse is hurtful or belittling language. Sexual abuse is any nonconsensual sexual contact.

43. B: An oral statement made outside of the courtroom and then introduced during trial is called a deposition. Depositions are supervised by the attorneys in the trial, typically without any participation by the judge. An interrogatory, also known as a request for further information, is a set of questions asked by one party in a suit to the other. An interrogatory is intended to clarify factual matters. The initial conference is a meeting at which the two sides negotiate the discovery process. A request for production is a demand for specific documents related to an impending case.

Copyright © Mometrix Media. You have been licensed one copy of this document for personal use only. Any other reproduction or redistribution is strictly prohibited. All rights reserved.

44. D: It is most likely legal to install hidden cameras in a dormitory hall. There can be no real expectation of privacy in the hall of a dormitory, nor in any other public space. If a person could reasonably expect privacy in a given location, it is most likely illegal to install hidden cameras there. For instance, it would be illegal to install cameras in a dormitory room, a hotel room, or a public bathroom.

45. B: When a cell phone conversation is recorded, one party to the conversation needs to consent. In most states, only one party needs to consent in order for the recording of a telephone call to be legal. However, there are some states in which the consent of both parties is required. With regard to cell phone calls, federal law states that only one party needs to consent. Private investigators must be aware of the rules in their jurisdiction to avoid accidentally breaking the law during a surveillance operation.

46. C: Both database companies and consumer credit reporting companies are subject to the Fair Credit Reporting Act. Database companies, as for instance LexisNexis, are only subject to the FCRA when they disseminate information to insurance companies, banks, and the like. The three primary consumer credit reporting companies in the United States are Equifax, Transunion, and Experian.

47. A: The National Association of Legal Investigators has modeled its code of ethics after the code of the American Bar Association. The ABA has composed a set of eight rules and sub-rules, known as the Model Rules for Professional Conduct. These rules touch on the relationship between the professional and the client, the roles of the professional as a counselor and an advocate, the protocol for transactions with people other than clients, the responsibilities of professional organizations, the protocol for acts of public service, the procedures for providing information about legal services, and the expectations for professional integrity.

48. B: Pen registers are used to record the numbers dialed for outgoing calls on a telephone. A trap and trace device records the number of incoming phone calls. The trap and trace device functions much like the caller identification feature on a phone, but without the knowledge of the person receiving the calls. Bugs and wires are covert listening devices. A bug is a microphone planted surreptitiously, while a wire is a cord attached directly to the telephone or other communications cable.

49. C: An attorney may reveal information about a client when doing so would help establish a defense against criminal prosecution or when doing so would prevent substantial bodily harm to the client. An attorney may also reveal information about a client when doing so would prevent substantial bodily harm to another person. An attorney may also reveal client information when this would prevent the client from committing a crime or fraud. On rare occasions, an attorney may be allowed to divulge information about a client in order to acquire legal advice about confidentiality restrictions. In most cases, private investigators are bound by the same standards for confidentiality as attorneys.

50. A: A subject will typically look up when he or she is recalling information. Most people will look either to one side or the other when remembering or making up a response. The habitual response of a person will vary individually, so the interrogator should ask a few basic questions at the beginning of the session in order to get a handle on the subject's routine. Noticing the movements of the subject's eyes is a good way to assess his or her

Copyright © Mometrix Media. You have been licensed one copy of this document for personal use only. Any other reproduction or redistribution is strictly prohibited. All rights reserved.

honesty, since these movements are involuntary. Indeed, most people are not even aware that the recall of information usually stimulates looking up.

Copyright © Mometrix Media. You have been licensed one copy of this document for personal use only.
Any other reproduction or redistribution is strictly prohibited. All rights reserved.

Secret Key #1 – Time is Your Greatest Enemy

Pace Yourself

Wear a watch to the Private Investigator Exam. At the beginning of the test, check the time (or start a chronometer on your watch to count the minutes), and check the time after every few questions to make sure you are "on schedule."

If you are forced to speed up, do it efficiently. Usually one or more answer choices can be eliminated without too much difficulty. Above all, don't panic. Don't speed up and just begin guessing at random choices. By pacing yourself, and continually monitoring your progress against the clock or your watch, you will always know exactly how far ahead or behind you are with your available time. If you find that you are one minute behind on the test, don't skip one question without spending any time on it, just to catch back up. Spend perhaps 45 seconds on the question and after four questions, you will have caught back up more gradually. Once you catch back up, you can continue working each problem at your normal pace.

Furthermore, don't dwell on the problems that you were rushed on. If a problem was taking up too much time and you made a hurried guess, it must be difficult. The difficult questions are the ones you are most likely to miss anyway, so it isn't a big loss. It is better to end with more time than you need than to run out of time. You can always go back and work the problems that you skipped. If you have time left over, as you review the skipped questions, start at the earliest skipped question, spend at most another minute, and then move on to the next skipped question.

Lastly, sometimes it is beneficial to slow down if you are constantly getting ahead of time. You are always more likely to catch a careless mistake by working more slowly than quickly, and among very high-scoring test takers (those who are likely to have lots of time left over), careless errors affect the score more than mastery of material.

Secret Key #2 – Guessing is not Guesswork

You probably know that guessing is a good idea on the Private Investigator Exam - unlike other standardized tests, there is no penalty for getting a wrong answer. Even if you have no idea about a question, you still have a 20-25% chance of getting it right.

Most test takers do not understand the impact that proper guessing can have on their score. Unless you score extremely high, guessing will significantly contribute to your final score.

Monkeys Take the Private Investigator Exam

What most test takers don't realize is that to insure that 20-25% chance, you have to guess randomly. If you put 20 monkeys in a room to take this test, assuming they answered once per question and behaved themselves, on average they would get 20-25% of the questions correct. Put 20 test takers in the room, and the average will be much lower among guessed questions. Why?

Copyright © Mometrix Media. You have been licensed one copy of this document for personal use only. Any other reproduction or redistribution is strictly prohibited. All rights reserved.

This test intentionally writes deceptive answer choices that "look" right. A test taker has no idea about a question, so picks the "best looking" answer, which is often wrong. The monkey has no idea what looks good and what doesn't, so will consistently be lucky about 20-25% of the time.

Test takers will eliminate answer choices from the guessing pool based on a hunch or intuition. Simple but correct answers often get excluded, leaving a 0% chance of being correct. The monkey has no clue, and often gets lucky with the best choice.

This is why the process of elimination endorsed by most test courses is flawed and detrimental to your performance- test takers don't guess, they make an ignorant stab in the dark that is usually worse than random.

Success Strategy #2

Let me introduce one of the most valuable ideas of this course- the $5 challenge:

You only mark your "best guess" if you are willing to bet $5 on it.
You only eliminate choices from guessing if you are willing to bet $5 on it.

Why $5? Five dollars is an amount of money that is small yet not insignificant, and can really add up fast (20 questions could cost you $100). Likewise, each answer choice on one question will have a small impact on your overall score, but it can really add up to a lot of points in the end.

The process of elimination IS valuable. The following shows your chance of guessing it right:

If you eliminate this many choices:	0	1	2	3	4
Chance of getting it correct	20%	25%	33%	50%	100%

However, if you accidentally eliminate the right answer or go on a hunch for an incorrect answer, your chances drop dramatically: to 0%. By guessing among all the answer choices, you are GUARANTEED to have a shot at the right answer.

That's why the $5 test is so valuable- if you give up the advantage and safety of a pure guess, it had better be worth the risk.

What we still haven't covered is how to be sure that whatever guess you make is truly random. Here's the easiest way:

Always pick the first answer choice among those remaining.

Such a technique means that you have decided, before you see a single test question, exactly how you are going to guess- and since the order of choices tells you nothing about

which one is correct, this guessing technique is perfectly random.

Secret Key #3 – Practice Smarter, Not Harder

Many test takers delay the test preparation process because they dread the awful amounts of practice time they think necessary to succeed on the test. We have refined an effective method that will take you only a fraction of the time.

There are a number of "obstacles" in your way on the Private Investigator Exam. Among these are answering questions, finishing in time, and mastering test-taking strategies. All must be executed on the day of the test at peak performance, or your score

Copyright © Mometrix Media. You have been licensed one copy of this document for personal use only. Any other reproduction or redistribution is strictly prohibited. All rights reserved.

will suffer. The exam is a mental marathon that has a large impact on your future.

Just like a marathon runner, it is important to work your way up to the full challenge. So first you just worry about questions, and then time, and finally strategy:

Success Strategy #3

Find a good source for practice tests. You will need at least 2 practice tests.
If you are willing to make a larger time investment, consider using more than one study guide- often the different approaPrivate Investigator Exam of multiple authors will help you "get" difficult concepts.
Take a practice test with no time constraints, with all study helps "open book." Take your time with questions and focus on applying the strategies.
Take a final practice test with no open materials and time limits.

If you have time to take more practice tests, just repeat step 4. By gradually exposing yourself to the full rigors of the test environment, you will condition your mind to the stress of test day and maximize your success.

Secret Key #4 – Prepare, Don't Procrastinate

Let me state an obvious fact: if you take the Private Investigator Exam three times, you will get three different scores. This is due to the way you feel on test day, the level of preparedness you have, and, despite claims to the contrary, some tests WILL be easier for you than others.

Since your future depends so much on your

score, you should maximize your chances of success. In order to maximize the likelihood of success, you've got to prepare in advance. This means taking practice tests and spending time learning the information and test taking strategies you will need to succeed.

Since you have to pay a registration fee each time you take the Private Investigator Exam, don't take it as a "practice" test. Feel free to take sample tests on your own, but when you go to take the Private Investigator Exam, be prepared, be focused, and do your best the first time!

Secret Key #5 – Test Yourself

Everyone knows that time is money. There is no need to spend too much of your time or too little of your time preparing for the Private Investigator Exam. You should only spend as much of your precious time preparing as is necessary for you to pass it.

Once you have taken a practice test under real conditions of time constraints, then you will know if you are ready for the test or not.

If you have scored extremely high the first time that you take the practice test, then there is not much point in spending countless hours studying. You are already there.

Benchmark your abilities by retaking practice tests and seeing how much you have improved. Once you score high enough to guarantee success, then you are ready.

If you have scored well below where you need, then knuckle down and begin studying in earnest. Check your improvement regularly through the use of practice tests under real conditions. Above all, don't worry, panic, or give up. The key is perseverance!

Copyright © Mometrix Media. You have been licensed one copy of this document for personal use only. Any other reproduction or redistribution is strictly prohibited. All rights reserved.

Then, when you go to take the Private Investigator Exam, remain confident and remember how well you did on the practice tests. If you can score high enough on a practice test, then you can do the same on the real thing.

Copyright © Mometrix Media. You have been licensed one copy of this document for personal use only. Any other reproduction or redistribution is strictly prohibited. All rights reserved.

General Strategies

The most important thing you can do is to ignore your fears and jump into the test immediately- do not be overwhelmed by any strange-sounding terms. You have to jump into the test like jumping into a pool- all at once is the easiest way.

Make Predictions

As you read and understand the question, try to guess what the answer will be. Remember that several of the answer choices are wrong, and once you begin reading them, your mind will immediately become cluttered with answer choices designed to throw you off. Your mind is typically the most focused immediately after you have read the question and digested its contents. If you can, try to predict what the correct answer will be. You may be surprised at what you can predict.

Quickly scan the choices and see if your prediction is in the listed answer choices. If it is, then you can be quite confident that you have the right answer. It still won't hurt to check the other answer choices, but most of the time, you've got it!

Answer the Question

It may seem obvious to only pick answer choices that answer the question, but the test writers can create some excellent answer choices that are wrong. Don't pick an answer just because it sounds right, or you believe it to be true. It MUST answer the question. Once you've made your selection, always go back and check it against the question and make sure that you didn't misread the question, and the answer choice does answer the question posed.

Benchmark

After you read the first answer choice, decide if you think it sounds correct or not. If it doesn't, move on to the next answer choice. If it does, mentally mark that answer choice. This doesn't mean that you've definitely selected it as your answer choice, it just means that it's the best you've seen thus far. Go ahead and read the next choice. If the next choice is worse than the one you've already selected, keep going to the next answer choice. If the next choice is better than the choice you've already selected, mentally mark the new answer choice as your best guess.

The first answer choice that you select becomes your standard. Every other answer choice must be benchmarked against that standard. That choice is correct until proven otherwise by another answer choice beating it out. Once you've decided that no other answer choice seems as good, do one final check to ensure that your answer choice answers the question posed.

Valid Information

Don't discount any of the information provided in the question. Every piece of information may be necessary to determine the correct answer. None of the information in the question is there to throw you off (while the answer choices will certainly have information to throw you off). If two seemingly unrelated topics are discussed, don't ignore either. You can be confident there is a relationship, or it wouldn't be included in the question, and you are probably going to have to determine what is that relationship to find the answer.

Avoid "Fact Traps"

Don't get distracted by a choice that is factually true. Your search is for the answer that answers the question. Stay focused and don't fall for an answer that

Copyright © Mometrix Media. You have been licensed one copy of this document for personal use only. Any other reproduction or redistribution is strictly prohibited. All rights reserved.

is true but incorrect. Always go back to the question and make sure you're choosing an answer that actually answers the question and is not just a true statement. An answer can be factually correct, but it MUST answer the question asked. Additionally, two answers can both be seemingly correct, so be sure to read all of the answer choices, and make sure that you get the one that BEST answers the question.

Milk the Question

Some of the questions may throw you completely off. They might deal with a subject you have not been exposed to, or one that you haven't reviewed in years. While your lack of knowledge about the subject will be a hindrance, the question itself can give you many clues that will help you find the correct answer. Read the question carefully and look for clues. Watch particularly for adjectives and nouns describing difficult terms or words that you don't recognize. Regardless of if you completely understand a word or not, replacing it with a synonym either provided or one you more familiar with may help you to understand what the questions are asking. Rather than wracking your mind about specific detailed information concerning a difficult term or word, try to use mental substitutes that are easier to understand.

The Trap of Familiarity

Don't just choose a word because you recognize it. On difficult questions, you may not recognize a number of words in the answer choices. The test writers don't put "make-believe" words on the test; so don't think that just because you only recognize all the words in one answer choice means that answer choice must be correct. If you only recognize words in one answer choice, then focus on that one. Is it correct? Try your best to determine if it is correct. If it is, that is great, but if it doesn't, eliminate it. Each

word and answer choice you eliminate increases your chances of getting the question correct, even if you then have to guess among the unfamiliar choices.

Eliminate Answers

Eliminate choices as soon as you realize they are wrong. But be careful! Make sure you consider all of the possible answer choices. Just because one appears right, doesn't mean that the next one won't be even better! The test writers will usually put more than one good answer choice for every question, so read all of them. Don't worry if you are stuck between two that seem right. By getting down to just two remaining possible choices, your odds are now 50/50. Rather than wasting too much time, play the odds. You are guessing, but guessing wisely, because you've been able to knock out some of the answer choices that you know are wrong. If you are eliminating choices and realize that the last answer choice you are left with is also obviously wrong, don't panic. Start over and consider each choice again. There may easily be something that you missed the first time and will realize on the second pass.

Tough Questions

If you are stumped on a problem or it appears too hard or too difficult, don't waste time. Move on! Remember though, if you can quickly check for obviously incorrect answer choices, your chances of guessing correctly are greatly improved. Before you completely give up, at least try to knock out a couple of possible answers. Eliminate what you can and then guess at the remaining answer choices before moving on.

Brainstorm

If you get stuck on a difficult question, spend a few seconds quickly brainstorming. Run through the complete list of possible answer choices. Look at

Copyright © Mometrix Media. You have been licensed one copy of this document for personal use only. Any other reproduction or redistribution is strictly prohibited. All rights reserved.

each choice and ask yourself, "Could this answer the question satisfactorily?" Go through each answer choice and consider it independently of the other. By systematically going through all possibilities, you may find something that you would otherwise overlook. Remember that when you get stuck, it's important to try to keep moving.

Read Carefully

Understand the problem. Read the question and answer choices carefully. Don't miss the question because you misread the terms. You have plenty of time to read each question thoroughly and make sure you understand what is being asked. Yet a happy medium must be attained, so don't waste too much time. You must read carefully, but efficiently.

Face Value

When in doubt, use common sense. Always accept the situation in the problem at face value. Don't read too much into it. These problems will not require you to make huge leaps of logic. The test writers aren't trying to throw you off with a cheap trick. If you have to go beyond creativity and make a leap of logic in order to have an answer choice answer the question, then you should look at the other answer choices. Don't overcomplicate the problem by creating theoretical relationships or explanations that will warp time or space. These are normal problems rooted in reality. It's just that the applicable relationship or explanation may not be readily apparent and you have to figure things out. Use your common sense to interpret anything that isn't clear.

Prefixes

If you're having trouble with a word in the question or answer choices, try dissecting it. Take advantage of every clue that the word might include. Prefixes and suffixes can be a huge help. Usually they allow you to determine a basic meaning. Pre- means before, post- means after, pro - is positive, de- is negative. From these prefixes and suffixes, you can get an idea of the general meaning of the word and try to put it into context. Beware though of any traps. Just because con is the opposite of pro, doesn't necessarily mean congress is the opposite of progress!

Hedge Phrases

Watch out for critical "hedge" phrases, such as likely, may, can, will often, sometimes, often, almost, mostly, usually, generally, rarely, sometimes. Question writers insert these hedge phrases to cover every possibility. Often an answer choice will be wrong simply because it leaves no room for exception. Avoid answer choices that have definitive words like "exactly," and "always".

Switchback Words

Stay alert for "switchbacks". These are the words and phrases frequently used to alert you to shifts in thought. The most common switchback word is "but". Others include although, however, nevertheless, on the other hand, even though, while, in spite of, despite, regardless of.

New Information

Correct answer choices will rarely have completely new information included. Answer choices typically are straightforward reflections of the material asked about and will directly relate to the question. If a new piece of information is included in an answer choice that doesn't even seem to relate to the topic being asked about, then that answer choice is likely incorrect. All of the information needed to answer the question is usually provided for you, and so you should not have to make guesses that are unsupported or choose answer choices that require unknown

Copyright © Mometrix Media. You have been licensed one copy of this document for personal use only. Any other reproduction or redistribution is strictly prohibited. All rights reserved.

information that cannot be reasoned on its own.

Time Management

On technical questions, don't get lost on the technical terms. Don't spend too much time on any one question. If you don't know what a term means, then since you don't have a dictionary, odds are you aren't going to get much further. You should immediately recognize terms as whether or not you know them. If you don't, work with the other clues that you have, the other answer choices and terms provided, but don't waste too much time trying to figure out a difficult term.

Contextual Clues

Look for contextual clues. An answer can be right but not correct. The contextual clues will help you find the answer that is most right and is correct. Understand the context in which a phrase or statement is made. This will help you make important distinctions.

Don't Panic

Panicking will not answer any questions for you. Therefore, it isn't helpful. When you first see the question, if your mind goes blank, take a deep breath. Force yourself to mechanically go through the steps of solving the problem and using the strategies you've learned.

Pace Yourself

Don't get clock fever. It's easy to be overwhelmed when you're looking at a page full of questions, your mind is full of random thoughts and feeling confused, and the clock is ticking down faster than you would like. Calm down and maintain the pace that you have set for yourself. As long as you are on track by monitoring your pace, you are guaranteed to have enough time for yourself. When you get to the last few minutes of the test, it may seem like you won't have enough time left, but if you only have as many

questions as you should have left at that point, then you're right on track!

Answer Selection

The best way to pick an answer choice is to eliminate all of those that are wrong, until only one is left and confirm that is the correct answer. Sometimes though, an answer choice may immediately look right. Be careful! Take a second to make sure that the other choices are not equally obvious. Don't make a hasty mistake. There are only two times that you should stop before checking other answers. First is when you are positive that the answer choice you have selected is correct. Second is when time is almost out and you have to make a quick guess!

Check Your Work

Since you will probably not know every term listed and the answer to every question, it is important that you get credit for the ones that you do know. Don't miss any questions through careless mistakes. If at all possible, try to take a second to look back over your answer selection and make sure you've selected the correct answer choice and haven't made a costly careless mistake (such as marking an answer choice that you didn't mean to mark). This quick double check should more than pay for itself in caught mistakes for the time it costs.

Beware of Directly Quoted Answers

Sometimes an answer choice will repeat word for word a portion of the question or reference section. However, beware of such exact duplication – it may be a trap! More than likely, the correct choice will paraphrase or summarize a point, rather than being exactly the same wording.

Slang

Scientific sounding answers are better than slang ones. An answer choice that begins "To compare the outcomes..." is

- 118 -

Copyright © Mometrix Media. You have been licensed one copy of this document for personal use only. Any other reproduction or redistribution is strictly prohibited. All rights reserved.

much more likely to be correct than one that begins "Because some people insisted..."

Extreme Statements

Avoid wild answers that throw out highly controversial ideas that are proclaimed as established fact. An answer choice that states the "process should be used in certain situations, if..." is much more likely to be correct than one that states the "process should be discontinued completely." The first is a calm rational statement and doesn't even make a definitive, uncompromising stance, using a hedge word "if" to provide wiggle room, whereas the second choice is a radical idea and far more extreme.

Answer Choice Families

When you have two or more answer choices that are direct opposites or parallels, one of them is usually the correct answer. For instance, if one answer choice states "x increases" and another answer choice states "x decreases" or "y increases," then those two or three answer choices are very similar in construction and fall into the same family of answer choices. A family of answer choices is when two or three answer choices are very similar in construction, and yet often have a directly opposite meaning. Usually the correct answer choice will be in that family of answer choices. The "odd man out" or answer choice that doesn't seem to fit the parallel construction of the other answer choices is more likely to be incorrect.

Copyright © Mometrix Media. You have been licensed one copy of this document for personal use only. Any other reproduction or redistribution is strictly prohibited. All rights reserved.

Special Report: Additional Bonus Material

Due to our efforts to try to keep this book to a manageable length, we've created a link that will give you access to all of your additional bonus material.

Please visit http://www.mometrix.com/bonus948/privinvest to access the information.

Copyright © Mometrix Media. You have been licensed one copy of this document for personal use only.
Any other reproduction or redistribution is strictly prohibited. All rights reserved.

Copyright © Mometrix Media. You have been licensed one copy of this document for personal use only.
Any other reproduction or redistribution is strictly prohibited. All rights reserved.

Copyright © Mometrix Media. You have been licensed one copy of this document for personal use only. Any other reproduction or redistribution is strictly prohibited. All rights reserved.